INVEST, FEEL GOOD AND MAKE A DIFFERENCE

BY RICHARD ESSEX

ISBN 978-1499170399

TO ALL THOSE WHO HELPED WITH THE
CREATION OF THIS BOOK

AND TO ALL THOSE WHO WISH TO
MAKE A CONTRIBUTION TO A HEALTHIER,
SAFER PLANET

CONTENTS

INVESTING FOR THE BIGGER PICTURE

Trust in our financial services and investment sector is about the lowest it has ever been. A survey carried out by Lloyds TSB in 2012 showed that confidence in the UK stock market was hovering at 29%. Hardly surprising given the endless procession of scandals that have hit the headlines over the last few years.

At the same time however a new desire is emerging from the investing public. Among many parts of the world people are starting to ask about investing more responsibly in the world they live in. For example, in 2010 a survey commissioned by UKSIF, the UK Sustainable Investment and Finance Association, discovered that 54% of all British adults expressed a desire to make a positive difference to the environment with their savings and investments.

Yet despite the sentiment take up in ethical and socially responsible investing is still relatively marginal. In the UK for example, investment via retail funds (this means individual saving plans) represents around 2% of the total investment under management. So why is the take –up so small given the desire expressed above?

You may be one of those people who want to make a difference because you recognise the many social and environmental challenges facing our world today, but certain factors are preventing you from making a commitment.

I genuinely believe we are at a turning point where investing this way need no longer be the domain of specialist investors but can really start to be accepted as a mainstream activity. In addition I feel we can alter the perception of investing so that it is no longer seen as a necessary evil but as something positive to be attached to.

In order to get to this point however there are eight myths about this type of investing that must be broken; eight myths that I would add are currently being broken by the genuine Socially Responsible Investing industry that is happening right now!

I have summarised these below and will deal with them in detail in the following chapters.

Before doing so I need to clarify some terminology.

SRI INVESTING

Investing and making a positive contribution to the world we live in has been categorised under a number of terms in the past. These have included ethical, green and sustainable investing.

This has caused a certain amount of consternation with investment professionals who want to reach a larger audience. It can also cause confusion among the investing public.

To be honest it's a problem we are still grappling with. For the purpose of this book however I have gravitated towards the term **SRI,** short for Socially Responsible Investing. This is partly for practical reasons in that it hopefully helps the text to flow more freely. **SRI,** however also seems to be more widely accepted across different spectrums. For example, SRI is accepted by both the US and UK retail markets and is a term being introduced to emerging markets. It is also a term accepted by the institutional investment sector.

So to be absolutely clear when I refer to **SRI** it incorporates any investment that, in some way, is making a positive contribution to the physical or social environment, upon which we depend for the future sustainability of our world.

BREAKING THE EIGHT MYTHS

MYTH ONE

MY MONEY WON'T MAKE A DIFFERENCE

Your money is already making a difference. Alongside government intervention we are already making dents in some of the World's most pressing challenges. For example, according to a United Nations report in 2012, investment in renewable power and fuels experienced a 17% increase from the previous year. In addition this investment has spread to far more countries, meaning more countries are now focussing on clean energy targets.

As the economy is becoming more constrained by environmental and social pressure those that are meeting these challenges head on are creating far more investment opportunities for you the investor.

MYTH TWO

I CAN'T GET A HEALTHY RETURN INVESTING THIS WAY

This just doesn't stand up. SRI funds, that you can access, will be investing in those companies that are meeting these challenges and these companies have a better chance of succeeding financially in the future.

These could be companies tackling issues directly, such as Scottish and Southern, who are now one of the leading renewable producers in the UK. Because of their innovative approach they are now able to offer a dividend of around 6%, which is helping to support a sustainable share price. Equally they could be companies like Marks & Spencer who are successfully moulding environmental and social sustainability into their operations, thereby benefitting financially. By achieving results such as cutting down food packaging by 20% they have helped to reduce their bottom line costs and improve profitability. This is being reflected in a share, which is paying a healthy dividend, well above the market average.

SRI fund managers will be investing in a mixture of companies that understand and care about their responsibilities. The kind of evidence above is showing that this offers a more financially sustainable return for you, the investor.

MYTH **THREE**

THE MARKET IS NOT MATURE ENOUGH

The SRI sector is no longer a fledgling industry. As far as individual investors are concerned the size of funds under management has increased significantly. To be specific SRI funds under management in the UK have grown from £312m to around £10bn over the last 20 years. This growth ignores the large increase in SRI exposure within the institutional sector. This includes occupational pension schemes, which are paying far more attention to this area.

Equally the range of fund styles have developed dramatically. In order to meet investor's differing preferences towards SRI there are a variety of styles available.

Additionally, there are a number of underlying factors that support a far more mature industry. For example, environmental technology is far more advanced creating many more cost effective processes. The National Renewable Energy Laboratory in the US issued a report in 2012 saying that costs could be reduced by as much as 30-40% over the next decade.

Finally we, as consumers, are far more educated and attracted to supporting the environment than we were a decade or so ago.

MYTH FOUR

I CAN'T SEE WHERE I'M INVESTING THEREFORE I DON'T FEEL ENGAGED

This fear is perfectly understandable given recent events in the financial sector. One of the spill-outs of the financial meltdown in 2008 was the realisation that so many market assets suffered from a complete lack of transparency. Extremely dangerous, as it turned out, as so much of this so-called wealth had no real underlying value.

In total contrast SRI funds depend on transparency for their success. In fact the origins of these funds derive from an investor's need to recognise that they are making a positive contribution. As a result there is a greater commitment by fund managers in this sector to communicate with you, the investor.

MYTH **FIVE**

I HAVE NO TRUST IN HOW MY INVESTMENTS ARE MANAGED

As the Lloyds TSB study (mentioned above) suggests, people's trust in investing is at an all-time low and there is good reason for this. A series of financial mishaps over the last decade has severely dampened the performance of the stock market over this period.

However just as financial mismanagement and poor transparency has created this lack of trust then more responsible and open activity will have the opposite effect.

The building of trust with investors is integral to the SRI industry. As a result SRI fund managers will carry out a more in depth research process, including analysis of environmental, social, and governance factors. Evidence is now showing that when this is combined with financial analysis a shareholding is more likely to achieve long term sustained performance.

Additionally behavioural finance research supports the view that investors, on the whole, are more concerned with longer term sustained performance.

MYTH **SIX**

I CAN'T SPREAD INVESTMENT RISK INVESTING THIS WAY

Other than just considering specific risk that applies to an individual company or stock, risk needs to be considered in a wider context when planning an investment portfolio. In particular research has suggested that a spread of asset class and investment style is important in providing a well balanced portfolio.

A criticism of the SRI sector in the past was that it did not offer this diversification. This is no longer the case. SRI filtered funds now can include a number of different asset classes, including shares, corporate bonds and property. In addition the range of funds includes a wide array of styles. These different styles mean that, as a SRI investor, you can invest in larger, more established, sustainable companies, as well as emerging companies who are making a more direct contribution to a more sustainable future.

MYTH SEVEN

I'M WORRIED ABOUT MOVING 100% IN THIS DIRECTION

It's still very rare for existing SRI investors to place all of their wealth in funds within this space. This is partly because this area is still developing and can't currently satisfy every investment requirement.

For that reason you should not feel guilty if you only invest a proportion of your money in this area.

The real challenge for the SRI industry is to move from the margins to the mainstream so that greater impact can be made on the social and environmental challenges that face us. There will be more effective change if broader exposure is obtained from the wider market rather than just concentrate on the existing, traditional, ethical investor.

MYTH **EIGHT**

I WANT TO LEAVE A POSITIVE LEGACY WITH MY INVESTMENTS BUT FEEL HELPLESS ON MY OWN

You don't have to feel you are on your own; on the contrary, you can become part of a movement. This is a movement that I believe is currently moving SRI from the margins to the mainstream.

The evidence suggests that SRI has now gone through the early development stages and a recognised movement has now been formed. Indications of the importance of supporting a sustainable economy can be seen in the way government policy is being framed. In the UK, for example, we have seen government initiatives like the Green Deal and Green Investment Bank both supporting the importance of a sustainable environment.

When you consider how much SRI investing has increased over the last 20 years (see Myth Three above) then you will realise that you are far from an extreme, far out, tree-hugger but in fact part of a growing, established, responsible movement.

I will now deal with each of these myths in more detail.

CHAPTER **ONE**

YOUR MONEY CAN MAKE A DIFFERENCE

IT'S FAIR TO SAY THAT THE VAST MAJORITY of us do not want to harm our planet for our children and grand-children. Yet the investment decisions we make today can have that impact.

Many people are now starting to recognise that they should think differently about investing. There is still however a disconnect with many people.

They can't see how their investment is going to make any positive difference to our physical and social environment.

POSITIVE CHANGES ARE HAPPENING

Yet we are starting to make a difference already.

If we take one of the major challenges that face us, the decarbonisation of the planet, significant changes are happening.

According to the United Nations Environmental Programme report of 2012 total worldwide investment in renewable power and fuels had increased by 17% from the previous year. This figure had now reached $257 bn, a six fold increase on the 2004 figure. Renewable sources have now grown to supply 16.7% of global energy consumption.

In addition the report points out that investment from the private sector was almost double that of the public sector.

Another major demand is improving the health of an ever growing population. Again major strides have been made. According to the World Bank child mortality (based on children dying before age five) has reduced from 13 million in 1990 to around eight million in 2012. Again private sector investment has been an important contributor here.

In order to make my point more succinctly I think it's useful to give more specific examples of where positive channelling of money has really made a difference.

THE VIENNA PLAN

The first example I researched was a result of a recent journey I made. My partner is Hungarian and last year we were travelling over to see her family. Because they live close to the Austrian border we flew to Vienna and on the drive from the airport I was surprised by the masses of wind turbines that are scattered around the Vienna area.

Later that evening I carried out some research on the origins of this discovery and un-earthed something far more significant. It transpires that back in 1973 Vienna put together a plan aiming to seriously change their energy mix to a more environmentally friendly solution.

As a result a Vienna-wide investment hub was set up and this was the trigger to attract investment from the public and private sector, but including funds from people like yourself. Yes of course there were hiccups on the way but in the long term the success has been staggering.

The Vienna region now produces over 60% of its electricity from alternative energy. This includes (in production ranking) Hydro-electric, Biomass, and Wind. Putting that into context the UK provides less than 10% from these sources. Correspondingly Vienna are achieving great reductions in CO_2 emissions.

REDUCTION IN LANDFILL IN UK

Another good example closer to home is the massive reduction in landfill due to vast improvements in green alternatives such as recycling. According to Defra (The Department of Environment Food and Rural Affairs) landfill from the residential sector reduced from 22 million tonnes in 2001 to under ten million tonnes in 2012. At the same time the recycling rate has increased from 11% in 2001 to over 50% in 2012.

This has real positive environmental advantages because landfill produces a number of gases, the most lethal of which is methane. Not only does methane creep into the ground helping to pollute rivers and ground water, but it's about six times more damaging than CO_2 to the ozone layer. This is not forgetting that landfill is an eyesore and the fact that in this country we are running out of landfill space.

The difference was made here due to a combination of public and private investment. Local authority tendering has contributed to the above significantly but equally private investment in recycling companies has also provided valuable input.

A GROWING MARKET

Contributing to these big challenges isn't just the remit of governments or large charitable donors. There is an ever growing body of commercial companies that are recognising their social and environmental responsibilities and as a result making major contributions. Significantly these are the very companies that you can invest in easily via your pension plan or your savings fund.

It is impossible to be precise about the sheer numbers of these companies that are out there in the market place. It is also difficult to be precise on how responsible a company is and whether it is making an overall net contribution.

One measure that we do currently have however is offered by the number of SRI indices that have been developed over the last few years. A good example would be the FTSE4Good Global Index that was established in the UK in 2001. The FTSE4Good Global Index incorporates companies globally that meet certain corporate ethical standards. In particular companies are researched and scored on ESG ratings (Environment, Social, and Governance). They have to show acceptable scores across the range of their activities.

As of October 2012 the index had 736 constituent companies and a market capitalisation of over 13 trillion US dollars. These constituents have been picked from the general FTSE World Global Index, which has 2870 constituent companies and a market capitalisation of over 29 trillion dollars. Therefore FTSE4Good represents 25% and 43% on numbers and value respectively.

MORE FUNDS

Most of us however would not want to pick and choose which individual companies to invest in. Instead we would want to rely on fund managers who can help us find the right balance between making a positive contribution as well as a positive return.

In this respect there is far more choice than there has ever been. According to EIRIS, the 'Ethical Investment Research and Information Service', the number of explicit retail SRI funds in the UK has reached nearly 100. This reflects a decent growth of funds as there were only about two dozen around 10 years ago. Funds under management have also increased considerably growing from 1.5bn to 11bn over the last 10 years.

It is also worth bearing in mind that the above refers just to retail funds. These are individual funds bought by single investors like you and I. In fact when we take into account other investments that we can access such as occupational pension funds the size of funds grows greater still. Another sign that support is growing in this area is the increasing number of financial institutions that are nailing their colours to the SRI mast. UKSIF, mentioned earlier, is a body responsible for promoting environmentally sustainable and ethical investments within the UK. The numbers of investment companies who are active members has increased from 14 in 1996 to 71 in 2011. These institutions include investment managers, banks and investment banks.

So there appear to be far more funds that are offering opportunities to contribute to positive change. The question is how can you contribute in the way you want to.

The answer is that most SRI funds will state quite clearly what their objective and approach is.

The traditional approach tends to be that of laying down fixed criteria of what is ethically acceptable and what is not. These screened funds may well satisfy those people who have very clear ideas on what companies they should support and what they should not.

However we are also seeing the emergence of funds with a more fluid outlook. These can include funds that are aiming at positive social and environmental themes. They can also include 'best of sector' funds, which simply invest in companies that are offering the most environmentally and socially sustainable strategies in their particular industry.

THE EXTRA DIMENSION

There is one extra dimension with these funds in my opinion. The fund managers who run these funds tend to be motivated and dedicated in the same way you are. They want a cleaner, safer planet but at the same time to secure a sustainable return for you. They know they really have to engage with both the companies they invest in and you the investor if they are to create a successful fund.

The Jupiter Ecology Fund would be a good example of a fund combining an environmentally sustainable theme with a high level of engagement. It was one of the first retail funds to tackle these issues and has been run by Charlie Thomas since 2003. As a fund dealing in the global stock market it has outperformed the market norm over the last 10 years. To be specific at the end of October 2012 it had achieved an average annualised return of 7.81% per annum, 2.15% per annum more than the MSCI World Index (Index that represents large and mid –cap companies throughout the developed world)

These results are achieved with a combination of active analysis and screening of its holdings together with an active engagement policy. Along with other funds within the Jupiter group, Charlie and other members of the sustainability team are involved in a number of shareholder meetings in which they vote on sustainability and corporate governance matters. For example between the 1st January and the 30th June 2012 the team had voted on 1374 meetings worldwide.

Many meetings such as these stimulate improved practices by companies. For example the FTSE organisation, mentioned previously, has stated that approximately 60% of their many engagement meetings have led to improvements in ESG disclosure and practice.

The image of the fund manager as a concerned stakeholder rather challenges the stereotypical image of the blinkered macho-style manager who is only concerned with financial bottom line at any cost. They see positive sustainable investments as being at the heart of what they do. In fact if you took this passion away from them they would lose the reason for carrying out their function.

This passion is reflected in comments made in an overview of another fund managed by Charlie Thomas, namely 'The Jupiter Green Investment Trust'. This overview states that 'investment in environmental solutions businesses is no longer a niche enterprise, but is rather about investment in long term structural growth of the global economy'

Another more indirect indicator of fund managers' commitment in this space is the long tenure they tend to have with their funds. Another good example of this is Ted Scott who has recently retired from the F&C Stewardship fund (this previously being the Friends Provident Stewardship fund). Ted helped launch the fund in 1984 and managed the fund solely from 2000 to 2010.

NEW SOURCE

I believe we will also see a steady increase of people who will want to manage their money in a more sustainable way.

New people coming into the industry are just a reflection of society as a whole. As we are seeing a younger generation growing up, more in tune with environmental issues, so we will see a growing stream of more enlightened people entering the financial professions.

I also feel that the younger generation are not held back by any negative hang-ups about environmental image. This view was supported during a phone call I had the other day with a research student carrying out a survey on buying behaviour with regards to ethical investments. During the course of the discussion I mentioned Swampy, that long-haired eco-warrior legend of the early 90's. I think I was trying to make the point that some people still see this as the face of the environmental movement. She had no idea who I was talking about and expressed surprise that this in any way should be a stereotype.

We are now seeing young professionals who are better educated on sustainability issues. Interestingly enough investment managers have always come from a variety of educational backgrounds. For example fund managers quite often have attained academic degrees such as History, English, and Philosophy. However as the environment and sustainability becomes more significant then more qualifications, such as degrees, will have this type of slant to them.

THE DEMAND HAS TO INCREASE

The simple fact is that the reality of environmental challenges combined with the emergence of political will can only lead to a greater demand for sustainable and responsible investment.

Extreme weather events, such as the recent Hurricane Sandy on US's East Coast, are helping to support the claim that global warming is having real impact now. In fact, according to Oxfam the number of people affected by extreme weather has doubled over the last 30 years and is expected to move from 243 million to 375 million a year by 2015.

This is also stirring governments to take on this issue in a far more responsive way than they have before. Whilst there is still some debate over the full cause of rising temperatures the weight of evidence claims CO_2 is definitely a contributing factor and that we are dangerously influencing CO_2 emissions now. Studies have shown that we have already reached a level of atmospheric conditions that is very close to that which will lead to a real risk of runaway climate change. Therefore governments recognise now that they have to instigate policies that reduce this risk.

In the developed world the G8 countries have set a reduction target in CO_2 emissions of 50% by 2050. The European Commission has set itself a target to reduce emissions by 20% from 1990 levels by 2020.

This means governments have committed themselves to encourage investment in cleaner, renewable energies.

Back in 2009 at the Copenhagen Climate Change Summit Dr Faith Birol, the Chief Economist of the IEA (International Energy Agency), was quoted as saying that 72 pence in every £1 of energy investment should now be directed towards renewable energies. In actual money terms they estimate this equates to around £10.5 trillion up to 2030. That's a lot of investment.

The UK set its own target of generating 15% of its energy supply via renewable energies by 2020. We currently generate about 2-3% from these sources.

Leaving aside global warming altogether perhaps a more immediate pressure comes from the stress on resources. For example there is now a large school of thought that claims that oil is quickly reaching its peak. For example in 2010 the UK Industry Task Force on Peak Oil predicted that we could reach peak oil by 2015 from which future levels of production will either plateau or begin to diminish.

Even where there are still significant reserves these are often too costly or dangerous to be viable. Jeff Rubin, in his book 'Why your world is about to get a whole lot smaller', gives the example of the Canadian Tar Sands Fields. He makes the point that the process of producing liquid oil from these oil clad sands is vastly more expensive than more established conventional means. He claims that an oil sand operator must spend one Btu (British thermal unit), for every three Btu's they extract from the fields. By comparison you would get 100 Btu's of energy back for that one spent on a conventional Middle East well.

Perhaps we can be slightly more optimistic but only if we take action now. We have to start investing now in alternatives, and investing in far larger quantities than we have in the past. We have to invest in alternative energies, alternative measures of fuelling and organising transport, as well as ways of conserving energy.

The same issues apply with our other basic resources; water, agriculture and forestry. They all play vital roles in providing the quality of life that we have today. We need therefore to seriously consider what would happen if these dried up.

So where will the investment come from to support this extra supply. Whilst government support has been important in supporting new technology in areas such as renewable energy the private sector is now becoming an ever more important part of the mix. Governments across the globe have been hit with significant budget deficits which have weighed far more responsibility on the private sector. One downside of this is that subsidies are no longer as attractive as they were. However this has partly been outweighed by the reduction in technology costs. For example Ernst & Young compiled research in 2011 to show that the cost of solar panels had halved since 2009.

So as technologies and industries are becoming more mature so will companies become successful and investors will benefit as a result.

YOU CAN MAKE A DIFFERENCE GLOBALLY

This demand is not just coming from the more established nations. It is coming in equal measure from the new power house economies such as China, India and Brazil.

There are often more immediate reasons why. India, for example, has a very strong case for favouring renewable energy. This is to do with its infra-structure. This was highlighted in a recent TV debate I was watching, involving environmentalists, businessmen and politicians from around the world. During the debate a question came up on how electricity demands can be met in emerging nations, such as India. A senior Indian businessman made a very interesting observation. He said that unlike the centralised electricity grid we have in the UK the Indian version is much more disjointed. In fact around 45% of the Indian population have no access to electricity at all, and these tend to be the poorest people living in rural areas.

As a result many renewable ventures are now taking place. Indeed India now has a 'National Action Plan' on climate change.

China is also starting to recognise the importance of more environmentally friendly technology not only from the environmental perspective but for sound economic reasons.

They currently have a 5 year plan including cutting its energy intensity by 16% and reducing water intensity per unit of GDP by 30%.

In 2009 Brazil pledged to reduce the rise in greenhouse gases by significantly cutting its deforestation rate including an 80% reduction in the Amazon and 40% in the Cerrado area. At the Durban conference of 2011 they announced they were on track to meet 65% of this target.

And it's not just in the field of energy where we can make a difference. Despite very rapid growth, emerging and under-developed nations still have exceedingly high pollution, ineffective waste management, and poor sanitation, and as a result huge amounts of poverty. Often these problems are associated with an imbalance of wealth between the rich and poor, which can contribute to social tension and unrest.

Governments and organisations are beginning to realise that we have a responsibility to encourage more sustainable investment overseas if we are going to make this a more equal and, ultimately, safer world for our children.

SOCIAL CHANGE CAN ALSO BE INFLUENCED

There is also a much wider recognition that investment must help to stimulate a better social environment. These would include health and wellbeing, working conditions, and of course basic human rights.

Often improvements in the physical environment will have a positive spin off on social conditions.

In fact many of the new economies mentioned above are seeing far better social conditions as a result of a better environment around them. In China, for example, there is a growing awareness that workers should have improved working conditions, and that they should not have to put up with the old sweatshops. A high profile example would be the conditions of workers at a company called Foxconn who are a main supplier for Apple. Following a number of incidents, among which were industrial disputes and even suicides, working conditions have been improved. These have included improving actual physical working areas, safety conditions, as well as reducing working hours.

But there are also good examples of an improving social environment resulting from sustainable investment closer to home.

A good example of social change influenced by investment would be that of social housing in the UK. There are now more developers and housing associations dedicated to providing sustainable, affordable housing, which in turn is improving social conditions for the people living there. What's more these organisations are seeking finance from private investors as the more conventional forms of financing are becoming more difficult to access.

In 2011 a developer called 'Places for People' were the first organisation to issue a retail bond to help finance their housing projects. The retail bond is a facility whereby investors like you and I can lend money to the organisation in return for a competitive interest rate. The yield for the 2011 bond was 5% which offers a healthy return above bank interest.

In this case the bond helps to finance a number of environmental and affordable projects. One such example would be the Riversgate Project, a part of the Walker Riverside development in Newcastle. This is helping to re-develop 107 homes which will be offered for shared ownership and affordable rent. Eventually the plan is to tackle all 7000 homes in the Riverside area, which were originally constructed to house ship workers on the Tyne. The housing is designed to create a more neighbourly and safe environment. It also more aesthetically pleasing and built to high eco standards. This is already having social repercussions. For example, for a number of years there had been a large number of people leaving the area. This exodus has been declining dramatically.

WHERE INVESTMENT HAS MADE A DIFFERENCE IN THE PAST

It may be that you still need convincing that your money will make a real difference in the future. There are however some great legacies from previous civilisations. At the time these were investments made in projects improving conditions, which have had a positive impact on future generations. I have picked two specific examples.

THE VICTORIANS AND MODERN SEWERAGE

At the beginning of the Victorian era large cities still operated with largely open sewers. In other words the extremely complex and structured system that we take for granted today was not yet in existence. But after the 'Great Stink of 1858' a group of engineers, under the leadership of a certain Joseph Bazalgette, were given the responsibility of linking London's sewerage system with literally thousands of miles of interconnecting tunnels.

At the time the original instigators were met with an extreme amount of cynicism. But a positive case was made and money attracted for the project to be carried out. Can you imagine our lives today without a modern sewerage system!

ROMANS AND ROADS

Anyone familiar with those icons of British comedy 'Monty Python' will recall that immortal line, "What have the Romans ever done for us?".

The point was made satirically because, in fact, there are a number of significant influences created by that civilisation. One of the greatest of these legacies was the construction of the road network.

We take it for granted today but imagine where we would be had we not inherited the Roman innovations in road construction and layout. At the height of their empire they had constructed 400,000 km of roads, for the first time being able to transport and communicate on a large scale. The roads themselves were constructed with stone, cement, and sand. They also incorporated drainage. In fact they lay the foundation for the modern road building we have today.

At the time this would have been seen as a long term sustainable development, and so it has proved. There was nothing short term about it, nobody was going to make money quickly out of this network. Instead they saw it as a necessary development to ensure they created better living conditions for their citizens.

SUSTAINABLE INVESTING MEANS A TRULY HEALTHY FUTURE

When we talk about being healthy what do we mean? Are we just talking about having enough money? Well, not normally. We are also talking about our physical health, our diet, our exercise, our level of cleanliness and so on. As a result therefore we strive, through our activities, to achieve improvement in these areas. For example, we buy food that is better for us, or we dedicate time to take physical activity.

So by the same token we can apply the same approach to investing our money. I would argue it's not just about increasing our financial pot, but improving this in line with better ecological and social wealth. It is thinking about investing in a more sustainable way. That is, not just sustainable from an ecological and social point of view but interestingly enough from a financial perspective as well.

This fresh approach is now spreading to more and more investment managers and is now influencing political debate. Research is being commissioned in these areas, such as the recent Kay review headed by Professor John Kay, whose remit was to see what could be done to transform the mindset of mainstream investment in the UK and give it a longer term perspective.

Therefore there has never been a better time for your money to make a positive difference. However it would be naïve to encourage people to invest unless there was a real sustainable **financial** return at the end of it. We do have to provide for our families, help support our pensions, pay for our children to attend university, and so on. I come from a big family and like you understand that family always come first.

An old and rather tired accusation aimed at SRI investments is that they carry some kind of financial penalty. On the contrary however evidence is building to suggest that investments that respect environmental and social sustainability will enjoy sustainable financial returns as well.

Let's now look in more detail at why investing this way can give you a healthy return.

CHAPTER **TWO**

SRI INVESTMENT IS MORE FINANCIALLY SUSTAINABLE

YOU CAN GET A HEALTHY RETURN INVESTING THIS WAY

YOU DON'T HAVE TO LOOK 30 YEARS AND beyond to be rewarded for a responsible investment.

There are some extremely powerful factors that suggest investing this way **now** makes financial sense.

Let's look at these in more detail

COMPANIES HELPING TO OVERCOME ENVIRONMENTAL CHALLENGES WILL BE LONG TERM WINNERS

We have already seen some of the mountain of challenges that face us environmentally; the need for alternative energy, the need to save energy, waste management and conserving our water supply more efficiently. Of course there are many more; retaining healthy sustainable agriculture and forests, improving the physical and social environment in our towns and cities. The list goes on.

Past evidence, however, has shown that we tend to find ways of developing technology to help overcome environmental challenges, and those companies at the forefront of this technology will prove to be successful.

And what happens when a technology solves a problem and becomes successful? In basic terms it means that companies in this area will start making profits, enhance their share value, and further down the line start paying dividends to their shareholders. If the paying of dividends becomes a long term trend then the share will appreciate even further.

This might sound a little obvious but this is what sensible long term investing in the market is all about.

This is perhaps easy to forget after all the recent crises that have surrounded the markets. The end of 2008, for example, has left a nasty taste in the mouth for people where they simply have seen the market as a casino for gamblers.

So let's break this down in a bit more detail and see how companies are benefitting from specific environmental challenges.

SUCCESSFUL COMPANIES WILL BE THOSE THAT BENEFIT FROM THE ECOLOGICAL CONSTRAINTS

We have already seen in the last chapter some of the targets facing the developed world.

As a result there is a very real desire to find solutions and make them commercially viable. This need couldn't be more relevant than when applied to alternative energy.

However, good news is at hand. We are starting to see real indications that companies who are developing in this area are showing real signs of future sustainable returns.

An example would be SSE Group PLC, previously Scottish & Southern. SSE are one of the UK's largest power generation providers who have made significant inroads into the renewable energy sector. In fact they have ownership interest in over 100 thermal and renewable power stations and are now Scotland's leading renewable producer. This has helped to reap positive rewards for investors. In particular their dividend payments have shown sustainable growth over the last 10 years. In 2003 the dividend per share was 30.5 pence. This has risen consistently over the last 10 years, outstripping inflation, up to 2013 where the announced dividend is 84.2 pence per share. Based on their share price on 1st January 2013 the dividend payment equates to just under 6% of share price value. Equally the share price has performed well over this period. Between 2nd January 2003 and 2nd January 2013 the share price increased by 115% when compared with a 50.39% increase in the FTSE 100 over the same period.

An overseas example would be the Elster Group based in Germany. They are benefitting from the constraints that face us with regards water and energy efficiency. They do this by providing advanced metering solutions and smart grid technology. They are now recognized as one of the major players in a high growth industry with operations in over 100 countries.

This can be seen from the analysis carried out by the NASDAQ market, the second largest American stock market, which Elster joined at the back end of 2010. In their summary of 30th January 2012 NASDAQ showed that Elster's earnings growth for 2011 was 33.24% against an industry average of 18.10%. They also show that the share price reflects good value given this level of earnings. Not surprisingly their analysts currently indicate the stock as a very good buy.

Both these stocks have been invested in by certain SRI collective funds.

EMERGING NATIONS CAN SEE ECONOMIC ADVANTAGES

I have had many conversations in the past with people about investing for the environment. One common response is 'what's the point us doing anything about it when the new emerging countries will simply ignore their responsibilities'.

But this is missing a significant point.

Countries like India and China don't have the same traditional infra-structure and industries that we have. They are starting from a newer base. Therefore in many ways they are far better equipped to take on new technologies, and new technologies that will have economic as well as environmental rewards.

A fine example of this would be the potential of the solar industry in China.

With the help of clear government planning, subsidies, and a lower cost base China has stolen a march on its western rivals and now become the largest world exporter of solar equipment. This has resulted in very sudden growth for the top companies in this area.

JA Solar is one such company. They are now one of the world leaders in solar cell production. Their growth has been astounding. Between 2009 and 2010 total revenues increased from $3.8bn to $11.8bn, a percentage increase of 211%.

It could be argued that these levels of growth cannot be sustained particularly as margins have recently been squeezed due to price pressures. As a result companies like JA Solar may have to diversify from being driven purely by exports. The signs for development however are encouraging.

China, for example, is planning to develop its domestic market. It has set itself a target that it will generate 15% of its energy from solar power by 2020. This would make it by far the biggest solar producer in the world. This then provides huge opportunities for companies like JA Solar to expand into areas like solar project development.

TACKLING SOCIAL CHALLENGES CAN ALSO BE FINANCIALLY SUCCESSFUL

There are now plenty examples of companies making healthy profits by finding solutions to social challenges.

One such challenge we touched on previously was that of 'Health and Well-Being'. With an ever ageing population there is now a greater demand for innovative, quality, medical care. One such company, very much at the forefront of this is Smith & Nephew.

Founded in the UK in the early part of the last century they are a world leaders in the provision of precision equipment for the medical industry, in particular orthopaedic treatment, wound management, and invasive surgery.

More importantly their continued success seems to be very much related to the social impact of their business. Their vision refers to them, 'helping people regain lives by repairing and healing the human body'. They also go on to stress the importance of the quality relationships they have with medical professionals and other stakeholders.

This socially responsible approach certainly seems to have helped Smith & Nephew achieve strong financial results. Firstly, since 1937 they have never failed to pay a dividend. This and other factors have resulted in real strength with regard to its share price. For example between 6th February 2002 and 6th February 2012 the share price increased by 60%. This compared with a 16% rise by the FTSE 100 (of which it's a constituent) over the same period.

Again, interestingly, this is a stock you can invest in through SRI funds.

SRI FACTORS ARE AFFECTING COMPANY PROFITABILITY NOW

But the SRI factors reach wider than those which simply apply to environmentally and socially friendly businesses. Studies are beginning to show that positive performance in these areas will be a real driver for better business value throughout many industries.

On such study was carried out by Jantzi-Sustainalytics, a renowned research house in 2011. It looked to see whether corporate competitiveness is linked to environmental and social impacts in the mining, oil and gas, and forestry sectors, (not exactly all environmentally friendly). They did this by establishing, through detailed research, what the main business drivers for success were. These consisted of internal drivers, such as operational efficiency and reputation and external drivers, such as access to natural resources and political environment. They then uncovered through empirical and analytic research how strongly these drivers were affected by social and environmental policy.

The key conclusion was that corporate responsibility performance has a positive impact on business success. In particular when an organisation's most significant environmental and social issues are addressed business value is created.

They also found that this correlation was strongest where multiple drivers of business were being impacted. In particular they found that if a company was addressing issues to do with reputation, operational efficiency, political and regulatory environment, and access to natural resources and labour, there was much greater chance of success.

There have also been examples in other business sectors where responsible sustainability has had a positive impact on profitability. Marks and Spencer (M&S) are a case in point when it comes to the retail sector. Over the last number of years they have embedded environmental and social sustainability into their everyday operations making it an important part of their long term growth strategy.

Two very practical ways that costs have been cut and profitability improved are as follows; food packaging has been reduced by 20% and their total logistical operations run on 20% greater fuel efficiency.

This strategy has played its part in making M&S a very attractive long term investment. This is supported by the fact that it's quoted dividend yield was 4.5% in 2012 against an average FTSE yield of 3.99%. (This was based on the M&S closing share price at 30 March 2012) and the declared dividend for 2012).

THE MARKET IS ALREADY REALISING THE IMPORTANCE OF THESE FACTORS

It's not however just independent analysis that is highlighting the importance of SRI factors. The stock market itself is already taking practical steps to underline their significance. A real centrepiece of this is the emergence of ESG (environmental, social, and governance) factors, mentioned in the previous chapter. Put simply it's a way of assessing a company's ethical footprint. Up until now the measurement of ESG factors has been somewhat an ad-hoc and subjective exercise. There are now, however, real signs that ESG is being seen as a universally recognised form of measurement.

Integral to this change has been the FTSE (Financial Times Stock Exchange) organisation, who in 2011, introduced their new ESG rating system. This will be a formulaic way of quantitatively measuring ESG factors so that asset managers can take these into account when analysing the value of potential stocks. These ratings are to apply to all 2400 stocks in the FTSE world all-share index. As Mark Makepiece, CEO of the FTSE, says in the 2011 FTSE4Good 10 year report, 'Our desire to provide ESG data solutions is matched by the rising interest of asset owners and managers worldwide.'

The market is also being affected in other ways. In 2000, for example, updated legislation came into place requiring trustees of company pension schemes to make a disclosure on its policy with regards responsible investing. This must state the extent to which social, environmental, or ethical considerations are taken into account in the selection, retention, and realisation of investments.

Despite there being some initial comments of lip service with regards this process we are now starting to see pension trustees apply real pressure on fund managers in respect of where pension funds are being directed. This is not least to do with the fact that trustees could be held personally liable if sustainability criteria can't be met.

Despite falling slightly in recent years institutional investment via pension funds still forms a significant proportion of the overall shareholding in this country. Therefore the attention to SRI engagement is building further market influence.

THE IMPACT OF ENVIRONMENTAL LEGISLATION ON COMPANIES

Whereas ten even five years ago this was perceived as a distant threat, it's now very real.

There are reams of legislation coming through that are putting demands on organisations. More significantly there is now real teeth if they contravene. This affects their standing and value, which more importantly can affect **your investment**.

So how is it having an impact?

Firstly it's significant to see the amount of legislation that is coming through.

If you take the ecological side alone the list of regulations is growing all the time. According to the regulation website sponsored by the UK Environment Agency there are eleven ecological categories, including energy, chemical control, waste and water management. Within each category there are scores of regulations and acts to abide by.

It stands to reason therefore that companies who are managing this barrage and fitting it into their structure will cope far better financially in the future. They will be spending far less time firefighting and more time being able to plan positively and strategically in the future. Investment managers, who are working for **you,** are also becoming increasingly aware of the significance of this. **The effects of non-compliance can be severe**

In the past an organisation perhaps needn't have been so worried about this type of compliance. This is no longer the case. There are plenty examples of situations where non-compliance can have very damaging financial effects.

Such an impact has been felt by Drax PLC, the owner of Western Europe's largest coal-fired power station based in Yorkshire. Between 11th June 2007 and 11th June 2012 the share price fell by just under 30% (source notes). More significantly in 2009 it was assigned junk bond status by the investment rating agency Standard and Poors, reflecting its poorer standing in the market. Whilst to some extent this was affected by a drop in wholesale electricity prices, much was to do with the cost associated with carbon emissions. For example in 2002 its total pay-out for carbon offsets was £11m compared with £223m by 2007.

In the UK, as a result of EEC legislation, companies are now having to comply with a piece of legislation known as the 'Carbon Reduction Commitment Energy Efficiency Scheme'.

This is aimed at large private and public organisations who operate mandatory ½ hourly electricity meters. The scheme requires them to monitor, manage, and record their energy usage. More importantly it requires organisations to buy allowances if they exceed carbon emission limits. Therefore there is a real financial incentive for organisations to reduce their footprint.

LONG TERM REPUTATION CAN BE DAMAGED

Whilst the financial consequences of non-compliance are painful it is the damage to long term reputation which is more significant. It could be very hard for an organisation to bounce back from serious reputational damage. This, it could be argued, is the situation surrounding BP.

The immediate reputational fall-out from the Deep Water Horizon disaster was severe. Both the ecological damage and associated human suffering was splashed across our TV screens every night. Consequently this has had financial implications. In the immediate aftermath of the disaster in June 2010 the share price more than halved, and at one stage bankruptcy looked a possibility. Admittedly since then the company has steadied the ship somewhat and its share price has rallied to recover some of the losses. However a big question mark still remains over the stock, once seen as a secure blue chip stock. Many analysts now see its risk/reward ratio as being too great to hold as a long term defensive type stock. This is not helped by the uncertainty still remaining over potential litigation costs in the US. The current commitment is seen to be around $37bn but the extent of the litigation could be greater still. As the Jantzi-Sustainalytics study uncovered, reputation is a key element in achieving sustainable profits. In particular the reputational hangover from drawn-out litigation, as with BP, could be extremely damaging.

It could also be argued that the reputational risk that companies like BP have suffered will have a positive effect on how organisations behave environmentally in the future.

The statement of intent is certainly there. For example if you go to the front page of any major energy company website you are likely to see a clear statement on environmental sustainability. Many commentators would argue that this is just paying lip service towards real environmental change. I would however make two points here.

Firstly, as seen from the examples above, they can now see the financial effects of non-action.

Secondly they know that investment advisers, and investors **like**

you demand more transparency with regards their environmental strategy. There is a growing recognition that potential stakeholders need to be reassured more effectively when potential environmental dangers come to light. Also as the stakeholders become more informed there is a recognition that any disclosures from organisations need to be more accurate. In other words the wool can no longer be pulled over people's eyes.

As a member of the Ethical Investment Association (EIA), I can provide a good example of the type of disclosure that is being produced. Over the last year or so I have started to receive a number of sustainability reports from major oil and energy companies. This suggests that they are now more willing to engage on environmental issues.

THE SRI INDUSTRY WILL MANAGE RISK ADJUSTED RETURNS BETTER

I talk to clients every day and unsurprisingly there is no great warmth expressed about the stock market. Hardly surprising when you consider some of the activities that have gone on in certain parts of the financial sector, and the damaging consequences that have resulted.

To sum up short term speculation and, let's be honest, gambling have caused havoc with the markets. In the short term, of course, this affects **our investments.**

I met up with a representative from a well-known fund manager the other day and he was giving me their house view of the short-term prediction for the market. His answer was, 'We haven't got a clue.'

And the point is that at the moment nobody has a clue.

There's all this nasty private sector debt accumulated in 2008, which has now been passed on to governments. Nobody seems to know how nasty some of it is and basically there is a load of knee-jerk speculation sending the markets up and down like a yo-yo.

But interestingly when I asked him about the long term the answer was different. In the long term his fund managers look at fundamentals.

And what are fundamentals? Well these are simply the factors that will determine whether an individual company is worth investing in. In other words is money coming through the tills and making a profit, and more significantly whether this profit can be sustained.

The market over the long term is still really quite simple. In fact if you look at behaviour of markets over the last 100 years or so there has always been volatility over the short term. (The graph below from the UK stock market Almanac 2013 clearly highlights this.) The markets, however, have always corrected themselves within a relatively short space of time. In other words the effects of speculation, on a fund price, only lasts so long. Eventually the price returns its attention to the fundamentals.

The question is therefore how can a company achieve sustainable profit, and thereby strengthen its fundamental price? Any experienced analyst will tell you that the key is how well that company protects against risk in providing this profit. This is often referred to as risk-adjusted returns.

In the past analysis on risk-adjusted returns would tend to be based on traditional economic and market risk. Now however there is a growing consensus that analysts must look at how organisations manage risk from the social and environmental dimension too.

This is because we are now starting to see a real link between the successful management of these risks and better financial performance.

In my view the sustained success of companies like Smith & Nephew, mentioned earlier, is in no small way connected to the strong social and ecological dimension that is characteristic in many of its policies and systems.

In a broader sense their attention to these areas provides reassurance to their customers and investors. An example of this would be that each global business unit within the company submits quarterly data relating to its health, safety and environmental policy. Another would be that many of its environmental management systems are accredited as meeting recognised international standards.

Often however a much more direct link can be seen between environmental policy and improved financial performance. Bottom line savings, for instance, have been achieved at their manufacturing plant in Suzhou China. Firstly a system has been devised for recycling the foam material that was an offshoot of a wound dressing that was being manufactured. Instead of going to landfill the foam is now being repackaged in furniture. This policy saved the company $200,000 in 2010. In addition a further $100,000 was saved by the employees adhering to a switch off campaign in respect of electricity use.

Whilst on their own these savings might be seen as fairly insignificant when you apply similar policies across the company as a whole this starts to create real extra value.

SRI FUND MANAGERS WILL ENCOURAGE BETTER RISK-ADJUSTED RETURNS

Companies are also heavily influenced by fund managers who are their main conduit to capital. They have to listen to fund managers and will be influenced by them.

Therefore when an SRI manager communicates with a prospective company he will be saying that his investors wish to receive a sustainable long term return whilst reducing ecological and social risk. This will then encourage those companies to improve their sustainability policies and systems across the board. In other words there is a constant cycle of support.

An interesting offshoot of this tends to be the low turnover of stocks in SRI funds. This is because fund managers will have much more conviction in the companies they are investing in. This is in turn places much greater confidence in the minds of those company executives. It means they can plan more strategically in the knowledge that they have this support behind them.

Further help and encouragement is being offered by analysis and research supported by SRI fund groups. For example a study was completed in April 2011 by two sustainability experts, Christopher Butz and Laurent Nguyen, on behalf of Pictet, a large Swiss owned asset management company.

The purpose of the study was to investigate how integrated financial and environmental risk management can enhance sustainable share value

Butz and Nguyen investigated why certain responsible investments performed poorly during difficult investment conditions whilst others proved far more robust, and as a result performed well relative to the market as a whole.

As a result they discovered certain financial factors that tended to lead to stocks vulnerability.

In particular they picked up on two significant trends.

Firstly there seemed to be a trend linking poor performance with excessive leverage. In other words those companies that were borrowing too much to support their growth were leaving themselves vulnerable.

Secondly they noticed that sudden expansive growth, often through mergers and acquisitions, tended to signal danger signs for companies in this sector.

Whilst this is not fool-proof, and indeed the study is ongoing, it does signify that companies like Pictet are developing some very refined models for identifying investments that will be truly sustainable in both senses of the word, i.e. **financially and ecologically.**

This research can be of real use to companies as well as us, the investors.

CHAPTER **THREE**

SRI INVESTING IS A MATURE ACTIVITY

YOU ARE NOT IN THE MARGINS ANY MORE when it comes to investing this way.

This is becoming a much more mature industry and there is real evidence to back this up.

We have already seen how the growth of SRI assets under management, as a whole, has grown substantially over the last 20 years. But it is significant to see how specific components of this market have grown and developed over the years.

RETAIL FUNDS

These are funds owned by individual investors. They can be accessed through various products such as ISA's (Individual Savings Accounts) and Personal Pensions. They are largely collective type funds in that you invest in a mixture of stocks, shares and other assets, which are managed for you by a specific manager.

In 1991 UK green and ethical funds accounted for £312 million. Today that figure is nearer £10 Billion. That represents approximately a 3000% increase.

The number of funds in this space has also increased dramatically. According to EIRIS there are over 100 funds now that fit within the SRI category. This compares with around 20 funds ten years ago.

But there isn't just a growth in the number of funds that you can choose from. There has also been significant development in the variety and styles of funds out there.

When the first funds started to come out they were based on a fairly rigid screening process. In other words the fund operates filters through which companies have to pass to be potential candidates for investment.

These early funds tended to follow a more traditional ethical route and tended to concentrate more on strict negative screening.

A good example of this was the Friends Provident Stewardship fund now managed by F&C, the investment arm of the newly structured Friends Life. The fund was launched in the early eighties and very much followed this traditional route.

The fund therefore screens out areas such as animal testing, alcohol and pornography. Like other funds however the Stewardship Fund would also have positive screening where companies would be included in the available universe if they were showing that they were making a positive contribution to the social or ecological environment.

But the whole space has moved on a lot from here.

For example we now have engagement funds. Rather than lay down very tight, strict criteria fund managers would engage with CEO's and boards to see if they could be successful partners in the future. So initially the fund manager would work with the company to assess where they were with regard to environmental and ethical strategy. The fund manager would then assess whether this was currently acceptable to them. Whether they took them on or not they would probably look to set some future aims with the company, so as to encourage them to improve their sustainable standpoint. There would then be a continuous engagement between the two parties.

A good example of funds in this area would be the Alliance Trust range of Sustainability Funds. Here they invest in companies that fit into 4 broad themes of sustainability, including good governance and health and well-being. Engagement therefore forms an important part of this strategy.

More recently however we have started to see the emergence of more themed funds. As the name suggests these concentrate on certain themes. These could be particularly attractive to you if you were passionate about a particular area. They also have the advantage of developing particular expertise within the fund management group. Such an example would be the 'Wheb Sustainability Fund.'

This encompasses 9 growth themes that are aimed at meeting 4 major challenges for society, namely resource scarcity, demographics, over-consumption, and globalisation. The themes include areas such as water management, health and wellbeing and education.

Therefore there are plenty of individual funds that you can choose from with a number of different styles to suit your particular stance. This is important. After all we are all different. We tend to have our own view on the best way to solve some of the world's biggest problems.

Like me however you might like to consider a melting pot of a number of styles. This can now also be achieved. You can now access portfolios or a fund of funds (as we call it) where an overall fund manager will be investing in a number of different funds on your behalf.

These portfolios also allow you to spread investments across different asset classes. This is because there are funds now which specialise in other types of assets other than shares. The development of these other assets has helped to spread your investment risk and evidence has suggested that spreading risk this way is likely to make your investment more financially sustainable in the long run.

DIFFERENT ASSET CLASSES

Originally the main asset you could buy into in this space was a share. In reality you would be buying units in shares but these units would be a reflection of the basket of shares the manager was holding on your behalf. The reason for this was because the share was the most likely form of raising capital for those original companies being invested in. The likelihood was that a number of these original companies were of a size that raising money through share distribution was the norm.

However as companies have developed and as the market has become more sophisticated the number of asset classes has grown. For example you can now gain exposure to these companies via corporate bonds. These are lower risk than shares because in effect you are lending money to these companies, and like any loan you would be receiving your capital back at the end of the term with interest paid to you in between. There is still some risk with these however in that capital will not be paid if the company goes bust and defaults on its loan.

In reality corporate bond funds will spread this risk by offering you a basket of these loans that are bought and sold on the market.

And the list of asset classes has increased further. You can now invest in property funds within this space, and even brand new developments like Exchange Traded Funds, known as ETF's. These are investment vehicles that track particular indices. And yes there are now indices that track environmental and ethical markets.

The FTSE4Good is a UK-based index, for example, that encompasses companies who meet accepted corporate responsibility standards throughout the global markets.

GROWTH IN INSTITUTIONAL INVESTMENT

However the likelihood is that many of us are already exposed to this type of investment already. This is because a number of institutional funds are already paying much more attention to these issues.

According to the National Association of Pension Funds (NAPF) the growth of SRI investment within occupational pension funds has now risen substantially. This change has been influenced strongly by organisations such as UKSIF (the UK Sustainable Investment and Finance Association). They helped pass through legislation that now forces large occupational pension schemes to provide a suitability statement within its annual report. Whilst some would argue that this can just be given lip service by the trustees the risks of not doing it are substantial. This legislation does have teeth and therefore this is really starting to get pension fund trustees really engaged with the whole sustainability issue.

However it's more than just having your hand forced. Institutions have their image and credibility to think about. This is becoming a significant factor in the growth of SRI investment within charities.

I thought it was particularly interesting in 2011 when the whole furore of the News of the World saga blew up. What particularly interested me was the number of organisations who quickly wanted to disassociate themselves from the disgraced paper. This included a number of their investors, which included a number of charities.

One was the 'Church of England's Ethical Investment Advisory Group', who sold their stake in News Corporation, worth nearly £2 million in August 2012.

This raised a significant wider point, and that is that Charities need to think much more carefully about where they are safeguarding yours and my donations. This is vital to their credibility as they are ultimately reflecting our principles.

The development of the investment industry in the environmental and ethical space has been welcome as it now enables charities to be able to engage far more deeply with how their money is being invested. They can now be positive in two ways. There is the charitable use of the money at the end of the chain, but also now the effects of the money whilst it's being invested.

In 2009 the Charity Finance Group, in conjunction with EIRIS, carried out a survey of its members. It found that 60% of its organisation that invested more than £1m had some sort of ethical policy. In addition they found that a quarter of these invested further than just negative screening but also invested in line with its charitable aims and objectives.

MORE PROFESSIONALS, MORE EXPERTISE

Not surprisingly as the number of SRI funds increase then so will the number of fund managers entering this space. But it's also fair to say that we now have greater expertise than ever before because many of these investment managers have been involved in this sector now for many years. They have grown in experience in exactly the same way as the industry as a whole. They have learnt to improve the way they do things for you, and as a result improve the chances of securing a healthy return for you. In addition managers in this field stay in this area because they have a passion for it.

There are also more financial advisers now dealing direct with clients in this market. The Ethical Investment Association, which represents Financial Advisers dealing in the SRI field, has seen a 370% increase in membership over the last 15 years . This also leaves aside the many IFA's, who are not members but are starting to get involved with this area. It's also significant that this sector is increasing when numbers of IFA's as a whole seem to be declining.

In addition we are seeing growth and development in other associated areas. These include consultancy, property management specialists, education, and also journalism. If we look at journalism for instance, there has always been a financial trade press but now we are seeing the development of publications dedicated to the SRI cause. A good example would be 'Blue and Green Tomorrow' an on-line and off-line publisher whose aim is to encourage increased SRI investment within the retail market. As well as providing a diversified canvas of news and insight to its readership they also provide direct assistance to SRI investment by providing a lead generation service to IFA's in this area.

This hints at why professionals will have more to offer in this sector. This is because there is more **cooperation** within the SRI sector than the traditional investment industry. This happens because there are a number of interested parties coming from slightly different angles, but with one common aim, that is to make the world a more humane and sustainable place to live. Because this common thread is such a fundamental driver to each of these organisations' goals it makes sense for them all to cooperate as much as possible.

In the UK organisations like UKSIF have been very effective in facilitating events where this type of cooperation can be achieved. For example, I recently attended UKSIF's 20th anniversary event at the House of Lords. During the course of the afternoon I had conversations with financial advisers, environmental consultants, an NGO worker and a politician.

Such harmony will only help to make the SRI campaign stronger.

MORE COMING THROUGH

The signs are also healthy that we will start to see more professionals coming through in the future.

At university level now we are starting to see far more courses that have an environmental or socially responsible slant.

Even earlier than that we are now seeing greater awareness being spread through schools. In a survey carried out in 2011 the Co-op found that 62% of all school children sampled said they wanted to learn more about green issues.

This is important as they will enter the adult world without all the negative stereotypes that we had. They will see these new areas of environmental management as being the only way forward, dare I say even cool!

YOU THE INVESTOR ARE NOT MARGINAL ANYMORE

But it's not just the products and resources out there that are moving this type of investing away from the margins.

You the consumer are no longer marginal either. There's no need to secretly hide in the corner. You can hold your head up, stick it above the parapet, and ask to invest this way with many others.

And there are many others. Again bear in mind the statistics gained in the UK by UKSIF. In a survey carried out at the end of National Ethical Investment week in 2010 they estimated that 54% of the population were interested in investing this way. That's hardly marginal is it?

I think a lot of this new found desire has come about because they see far more credibility in the industry but they can also see that the typical environmental consumer has changed. We now have completely different role models from the old eco-warriors we had in the past.

Take the electric car for example. This has moved from being a slightly comical novelty item to a serious product. Whilst the engineering can take some of the credit for this, much also has to do with the advertising and promotion which is now surrounding it.

Perhaps the best example of this is the advertising surrounding the Toyota Lexus hybrid. This has been promoted as a very chic motor car, with none other than Kylie Minogue sitting at the wheel. I believe these messages are beginning to resonate at a general level with consumers who are concerned about the environment. This will include investors.

Potential investors can also take heart that politically green issues are moving more into the mainstream. Issues like carbon emission targets are right at the heart of political debate now influencing policies, such as the 'Green Deal', to come forward.

We are now used to seeing politicians from the major parties talk about environmental issues. In addition we are seeing the political spectrum widen. More overtly environmental parties, such as the Green Party, are having more influence in the UK.

At the beginning of 2013 they have their first Westminster MP in Caroline Lucas and hold over 100 seats amongst the many local authorities in the UK. Amongst these are authorities like Brighton, where the Greens are the majority party and are therefore strongly influencing local policies.

Some people might consider the Greens as being too radical. Whether you agree with this or not I think this emergent force is having a stronger influence on the mainstream parties.

UNDERLYING TECHNOLOGY AND INFRA-STRUCTURE IS MORE MATURE

I'm going to use a rather simple and perhaps crass analogy and refer to the environmental industry as emerging from its teenage years.

In other words it's had its really difficult early growing years and is now starting to show maturity, which in economic terms means a healthy robust future.

Not least is this the case with environmental technology. For example 30 years ago wind turbines were very much in their infancy. As with all new technologies you can imagine the reaction of the traditional energy market when these first came on the scene. 'What we're going to produce electricity from a windmill?'

In the 80's a commercial wind turbine would have generated enough energy to meet 25-30 homes over the year. The modern turbines today can cater for up to 1000.

It is also widely accepted that modern technology can help deliver cost efficiencies as well. According to a report in the US by the National Renewable Energy Laboratory we could be looking at 30-40% improvements in cost effectiveness over the next 2 decades.

As with other renewables Wind is not seen as the answer to all our energy problems but better reliability and performance will mean it's an important part of our overall energy mix

MORE MATURE INFRASTRUCTURE

Whilst technology is vital surrounding infrastructure has to be put in place to support it. There is real evidence that this works.

The area of clean energy very much supports this case. This is an area where the blueprint has been laid down in parts of continental Europe.

Such an example would be the Vienna plan that I mentioned earlier in my book. To restate back in 1973 the City of Vienna realised that it had to change its energy mix to meet the environmental challenges that were coming their way. As a result the governing bodies had the foresight to devise a co-ordinated strategy, involving the public and private sector. After a considerable amount of revision and a number of heartaches Vienna is now able to boast that approximately 65% of its electricity is generated from renewable energy.

Eco towns are another good example of infrastructure working hand in hand with technology. The other day I met a very dynamic young lady, who had helped work on the development of Freiburg in Germany, now voted the world's greenest town.

Freiburg is now heavily built from sustainable materials, has low emissions, and public transport that is the envy of the developed world. In fact the centre is a car free zone. But this didn't just happen by accident. There again had to be a co-ordinated plan in place. This was led very much by the city council and leading officials.

COMPANIES HAVE MATURED

Finally companies themselves have also matured. They have grown in size and status. Many companies that were once in early development stage are now leaders within established stock markets.

One such company would be the Sunpower Corporation based in California. They are now a global leader in solar technology having joined the Nasdaq stock market in 2005. But the company was only incorporated in 1985 and during the 90's was seeking early development finance from vehicles such as venture capital.

THE ENVIRONMENTAL IMPACT OF YOUR INVESTMENTS HAS IMPROVED

The impact of your investment in SRI activities can make more difference now as these activities are operated far more professionally than they were before.

Sustainable forestry investments provide a good example. If managed right re-forestation schemes can be a particularly helpful to the environment as well as also securing a healthy return on the timber. However the quality of these has developed significantly over the years.

In the past, and to some extent today, there has been a tendency to reforest by way of a monoculture. This means that whilst reforestation was protecting the ozone layer it was not fully respecting the wild life and plant life that lived within it. Bio-diversity, as we call it, is now very much part of the SRI screening process. The investment industry can now boast experts like who provides specialist advice and consultancy to these types of projects.

Therefore by investing in the right quality funds in this area you will be creating much more positive change than you had in the past. Better environmental impact could also now be aimed at more socially driven industries.

One area close to my heart is the growth and development of the cycling industry. This industry has experienced tremendous growth helped in no small part by the positive solutions it offers with regards health and the environment.

In 2011 a report from the London School of Economics found that £51 million was raised from UK manufacturers representing a rise of 28% on number of cycles sold in the previous year.

It is now recognised that the growth of cycling is not only hugely beneficial to your health but also has very positive social ramifications. Cities like Portland in the US have benefitted hugely from growth in cycling and the surrounding infrastructure. It has reduced pollution and congestion. It has made the city safer and road deaths have been reduced. It has made its populace healthier, and last but not least it has made the city a fun place to be.

It is now good to see cities like London, with Boris's bike scheme, follow the lead.

This has been a terrific boost to the cycle industry, as seen by the figures above, and of course anyone wishing to invest in it.

THERE IS NOW MORE GLOBAL COOPERATION

The development of truly sustainable industry and its associated investment has been helped significantly by far greater global cooperation.

Three factors have contributed to this.

Firstly there has been significant activity at international government level aimed at finding solutions to the great environmental challenges of the day. The Kyoto summit back in 1997 was obviously a pivotal point of much future cooperation. The global warming targets set there formed much of the backdrop for subsequent discussions and agreements. But negotiations at government level tend to have significant spin offs for the corporate level.

Secondly at a corporate level there are now numerous international trade exhibitions and conferences allowing companies from different nations to share ideas and technologies.

These have been of particular use to developing and emerging nations, who have needed to take on board new technology quickly to meet the massive increase in demand.

In China, for example, they have very much benefitted from taking tried and tested technology from Japan and Europe and innovating it to meet their own specific requirements. The growth of the high speed train industry is a case in point.

Part of the revolution over there has involved migrating a huge number of people from the countryside to the cities. As a result public transport has been an area that has needed to grow rapidly. In particular the new fast electric trains have been recognised as being effective, whilst at the same time friendly to the environment.

In addition certain conditions in these emerging nations have made it ideal to adopt some of the established technology. Making use of the disparate grid system in India by promoting renewable energy is a case in point.

So there is no need to be afraid you can invest positively, be successful with your return, and not be in the margins.

In fact that's what's really exciting about this type of investing. It offers you, the investor, a new mindset. You can really start to feel good and involved in your investment rather than a rabbit in headlights, which is what many investors have felt like in the past.

CHAPTER **FOUR**

YOU CAN SEE WHERE YOU'RE INVESTING

MANY YEARS AGO I WAS ATTENDING A SEMINAR hosted by a well know fund manager. This was held shortly after the exposure of Enron and the resulting market collapse. One particular manager was providing a summary of the economic situation and how it was going to effect markets and investments generally.

We had had all the usual charts and predictions, and I think by that stage I was getting a little weary, bored probably. To be frank I was getting tired of hearing that negative message that there is nothing we can do about the markets, in other words 'we'll just have to trust we make the right bets.' Something then jolted me out of my slumber.' I asked whether these sudden shocks to the markets could be avoided by investors having more information on where there funds are invested. I couldn't believe the answer. Basically the response was 'our view is that people aren't interested.'

Well aren't you?

And that was then. This is now. I wonder if that same manager would make that comment in the light of the financial meltdown of 2008 and its current repercussions.

The one over-riding lesson for me about 2008 was the complete lack of transparency of where your and my money was. Ok the house of cards may have been triggered by vulnerable US homeowners defaulting on mortgages but the situation would not have escalated to where it was if dodgy loans were not wrapped up in bigger dodgy loans, and then passed on into even bigger, dodgier financial packages. If people, with authority and without a selfish interest, had provided a culture of real transparency we would not be in the mess we are in today.

A staggering fact that came out of this mess was the excessive growth of derivatives.

For those of you who are not quite sure a derivative is an investment derived from something else. Hence you are not investing in a real asset rather a bet that is derived from the change of value in a particular underlying asset.

Derivatives do have a part to play. Their origins come from the Chicago agricultural markets in the 1850's where they were a very effective insurance allowing farmers and traders to benefit from steady prices and not be subject to the perils of unpredictable harvests.

They still have a very important part to play in this regard. But derivatives have been abused! People saw these as a great opportunity to make money quickly, greed in other words. They could wrap up, often very vulnerable, financial assets in a clever package and sell them on, making a quick buck in the process. The whole point was to hide as much of this as you could. And this happened time and time again contributing to a mountain of toxic debt.

You have probably heard all this before but it's worth quoting the numbers.

Apparently the size of the derivative market in 2008 was greater than actual world GDP. That is greater than the value of everything the world produces in that year. In fact according to distinguished sources, including the 'Bank of International Settlements' in Basel it dwarfed GDP by a multiple of 22!

So should you be interested in where your money's being invested? Too right you should.

But even where your pension and investment funds are invested in real stocks and shares of real companies, transparency is still vitally important.

Take the situation of Enron. Enron was a large US multi-global company when it collapsed. Despite having its origins as a gas pipe laying company their adventurous CEO, now prisoner Kenneth Lay, decided to change the company in the 1990's to a global trading company. Basically they would trade anything, moving away from their traditional origins. Unfortunately greed took over and accounts were distorted to report profits far in excess of what was really coming through the tills. But this was bought by the many fund managers who invested in them, including a number of leading UK pension funds.

So greater transparency is definitely needed.

Interestingly enough the origins of the ethical and
environmental investment sector have been built on the concept
of transparency.

The initial drive to set up this sector came from pressure groups.
These were groups of people fuelled by specific ethical beliefs.

The origins of one of the first funds in this area 'The Friends
Provident Stewardship' fund is a good example. Up until the
1980's the Friends Provident Board had a significant
representation from Quakers, who had originally set up the
company in 1832. In the early 1980's the Board were expressing
concern about how the company's funds should be invested. As a
result the Stewardship Fund was launched in 1984 to be
supervised under a specific 'Committee of Reference'. A leading
member of this Committee was a man called Charles Jacob. Jacob
is seen by many as the father of ethical investment in the UK.
With a combination of fund management experience and a strong
Methodist background he had been promoting and managing
money ethically for many organisations over many years. Jacob
became a founding member of the 'Committee of Reference' and
in fact founded the term 'Stewardship' based on a reference
relating to the right use of money as contained in the Bible.

In practical terms this meant that potential holdings were
screened out if they were involved in particular activities, such as
production of tobacco or alcohol or the unnecessary harming of
animals. Equally stocks would be positively favoured if they were
improving the ecological or social environment in some way.

This became a blue print for many ethical funds and as a result the fund managers became extremely aware of the impact their investments would have. In fact there emerged an awareness that they needed to notify clients where they were investing and reasons for doing so. Without this process in place they knew that trust would be broken.

So funds in this sector now rely on being transparent. They can't afford not to be, and it's not without difficulties.

I was at an EIA meeting not long ago. A fund manager was being quizzed on a share in his fund belonging to a well-known supermarket. Despite the audience being happy with some of the company's green policies they were grilling him on their policy towards chicken production. There is no need to go into the rights and wrongs but the point is that the manager had to provide very detailed information on the company's operations. I would argue that demand for this information is not as comprehensive in the conventional sector.

There is a more positive way of looking at this however.

INVESTMENT COMPANIES OFFERING POSITIVE SOLUTIONS IN THIS AREA WILL WANT TO BE TRANSPARENT WITH YOU

These companies often want to help solve fundamental problems with the environment, so it makes sense that they want to talk about it.

Their fact sheets will often be considerably more comprehensive than their conventional counterparts. The conventional fund will typically offer a fact sheet with limited information on funds, a list of the top ten holdings for example.

Eco and ethical funds on the other hand tend to produce far more detailed fact sheets. They will often include short biogs on the funds they are investing in. And far more detailed information is available if requested. Interestingly the Wheb Sustainable fund, mentioned earlier, is the first fund to actively promote the idea of revealing all its holdings at any time with a description of why it's doing so.

Equally I have found that fund managers in this sector respond quickly if you challenge something in their portfolio. This is a refreshing change from the typically more secretive world of the city.

I had first-hand experience of this when I recently wrote to a manager questioning its support of a well-known FTSE 100 stock. Whilst the company had been involved in promoting projects in the eco and social sector, there had been a question mark over some involvement that it had in the pornography industry.

I didn't just get a quick curt response. Instead I received a detailed reply on their current position with the company and what action they were currently taking with the company to see whether this involvement had any real substance in it and whether financial support could continue. This was refreshing and also gave me information from which to hold them to account in the future.

But rather than just receiving information with investments in this sector you can benefit from seeing real tangible benefits leading from your investments, not just the financial return that would result.

THE ENVIRONMENTAL AND SOCIAL INDUSTRIES CAN PROVIDE IDENTIFIABLE TANGIBLE BENEFITS

There are several specific reasons behind this.

Firstly within the environmental sector very clear targets are set, which need to be measured against. These targets and their subsequent measurement are often in the public domain.

Take the area of recycling, for example. In the UK, particularly in the domestic arena, this has really taken off now. We are all very use to going down our local tip where we are hit immediately with signs saying where we are with regard the local recycling targets, and more importantly, how much we are diverting away from landfill.

This has repercussions for companies operating in this area, and indeed the likes of you and I investing in them. For example, recycling companys' financial success will run very strongly with hitting recycling targets.

This is particularly the case in the UK where these companies have contracts with local authorities and will have to renew these contracts every few years. The keeping of these tenders will often be fundamental to the continued success of a company in this area.

Veolia, for instance, won their first refuse collection contract in the UK in 1990 and by September 2006 had become the recycling and waste management leader.

Then there is of course the many targets that exist in the energy field. As we have already seen CO_2 targets are only going to become more demanding. Also we are now seeing more stringent targets appearing with regards to our energy mix. This again is being passed down to the companies operating in this sector and again forms very much part of their success story.

Many energy companies now will state how they are meeting energy targets. These are high up in their list of priorities. This is because it can have such an effect on their valuation if they don't. The downgrading of Drax, discussed earlier, highlights this point.

Also however we can start to see a correlation between meeting such targets and their financial success.

Scottish and Southern, mentioned earlier, have set out in their energy strategy that they wish to reduce the carbon dioxide intensity of their power stations by 50% between 2005 and 2020. There is a belief there that a future sustainable energy policy is helping to contribute to its sustainable financial growth, particularly in relation to its dividend policy.

But sometimes the measurement against targets can be a little abstract.

It's nice to smell the roses so to speak. In other words it's important to be able to see and feel the effects you are having.

YOU CAN SEE AND SMELL POSITIVE CHANGES

Whilst wind turbines and solar panels may not be everybody's cup of tea I think most people would agree that this is far more preferable than huge coal based power stations bellowing out fumes. Slowly in this country we are seeing the landscape change as alternative energy replaces it's uglier more conventional counterpart.

And if you're not seeing change quickly enough here then just take a trip across the channel to see the positive effects of this type of investment.

The impact of the Vienna plan mentioned earlier is a case in point. Having driven through this area I saw no coal based power stations or Gas containers, or any resulting pollution. Instead there were thousands of wind turbines, which actually blended in with their surroundings. In addition they produced absolutely no pollution or noise come to that.

Equally an area like sustainable waste management has immediate positive side effects. In particular many countries in the developed world are increasing positive waste solutions, such as recycling at the expense of landfill. No more starkly has this been shown than in the case of the Netherlands. According to the Dutch Waste Management Association, in 1985 50% of their waste was disposed of in landfill. By 2007 this figure was reduced to 3%. There are of course long term effects to this, such as the reduction in carbon emissions that come from these sites. More immediately beneficial to the surrounding population however has been the reduction in more short term effects, such as groundwater pollution, resulting odour, as well as improving the visual landscape.

Additionally whilst these environmental effects are more evident in the mature economies, just imagine the potential improvement in the new economies of India and China where pollution has reached extreme levels in many areas.

YOU CAN SEE POSITIVE CHANGE IN SOCIAL ENVIRONMENT

And it's not just in the physical environment where you can see positive results. We can see more immediate improvements where we are investing in real social change.

The area of health and well-being is a prime example. Companies like Smith & Nephew, mentioned earlier in the book, offer excellent investment prospects, while also offering evidence of the lives they improve.

And now, for more sophisticated investors, you can have even more direct involvement with socially sustainable investing. This has come in the form of the 'Social Impact Bond'.

This really is a new type of thinking when it comes to investing, but makes perfect sense. It works like this.

An organisation will offer you the chance to invest in them and your return will be directly linked to positive social outcomes that are achieved by that organisation. Still confused? Let me give you a real example.

A group of organisations, including the St. Giles Trust, were asked by the Home Office to look at improving probationary work and re-offending rates at Peterborough prison. St. Giles Trust, for example, had some new, well researched strategies aimed at improving re-offending rates. However they needed additional funding to provide this service. So they requested this investment in the form of a Social Impact Bond. In their case they would offer you, the investor, a healthy return on your money if they were able to reduce re-offending rates to certain levels.

They will in effect receive their reward from the government, if these targets are met, because of the huge savings that are made if people don't have to be housed again in prison. To balance this out the investor could of course lose their money if targets are not reached.

In fact this is still a very new area and the Financial Conduct Authority (FCA), still see this as a highly risky investment and only suitable for sophisticated and high net worth investors (that is someone earning more than £100,000 per annum or with £250,000 capital available)

However the scheme is now being replicated in other social areas and over time proponents are hoping that this type of investment will become more tried and tested. There is therefore a blueprint now for being indirectly involved with improving someone's life chances whilst securing the possibility of a return on your investment, albeit currently with the risks, mentioned above.

FUND MANAGERS ARE PASSIONATE ABOUT SHOWING YOU WHAT THEY ARE DOING

So this type of investing offers a new dimension. It allows you to be involved in the investment. And being involved you are more than likely to know what is happening with regards to your likely financial returns.

This doesn't just happen by accident however. As I stated earlier this sector was built on transparency and this still is the case.

This comes about because the fund managers investing the money on your behalf are passionate to show what they can do for you.

This is partly due to the remit placed upon them. What do I mean by that?

All investment funds have some sort of objective they set out to achieve. In the conventional sector however this will often be a broad benchmark it has to keep to, in other words it will be restricted into what asset classes it invests in. No other demands will be made on it however.

With SRI investing however the funds will have far more specific and emotive remits. Whether it's due to specific screening or whether it's based on certain themes these remits will engage the managers more. This is because they will be aware that environmental and social outcomes are important as well as financial.

Because of these wider fund remits managers will have to account for these with much more comprehensive reporting on its investment process. This can manifest itself in several ways.

Fund prospectuses for example, inviting in investors, have to be more detailed in showing a fund manager's credentials. Annual reporting on funds is also important to show that investment parameters are continuing to be met.

This is particularly important to institutional fund managers. These are people managing your pension funds, who are now obligated by law to provide annual sustainability reports.

But if managers were just forced into these positions we wouldn't be seeing the sea change we are.

The reason that this sector is really different is that fund managers are proud and passionate themselves about making a difference.

For the same reason that I get up in the morning and am motivated to promote this way of investing, so are the fund managers in this sector.

If you talk to most of the successful fund managers you will find they didn't just fall into these roles. Instead they had a particular motivation to enter this field. They are human like you and I and they are concerned for their childrens' futures, just as you are. The difference is that these individuals believe that they can transform these environmental goals into financial ones.

Claudia Quiroz is the manager of the Quilter Cheviot 'Climate Assets Fund', a fund investing around the theme of climate change and resource scarcity. When I asked her what motivates her in running the fund her response was as follows;

"Every day when talking to clients and colleagues I see more and more interest in sustainable investing. There is no doubt in my mind that this is a growing investment theme."

She also goes on to say that "from a professional viewpoint it is exciting that we are now at an inflation point and these investments are not just for the good of the planet. They are being made because of the cost reductions they offer to the consumer, particularly in the area of energy efficiency and consumption with smart metering and insulation for example".

But I have also picked up on a further factor that I have noticed with this new breed of fund managers. They are much more willing to communicate with you the investors. Again this is a reflection of their passion and their understanding that you the investor demand transparency for these types of investments.

This manifests itself in a number of ways. I have already

provided an example of a fund manager responding comprehensively to a query relating to stock selection. Now fund managers are aiming to be more accessible through other mediums, such as on-line blogs.

There is even a movement now to bring potential investors and fund managers into the same room together. Imagine that.

I have always considered it strange that fund managers have kept themselves at arm's length from the people whose money they are investing. Whilst in the past they have been prepared to talk to advisers such as ourselves there has been a reluctance to speak to the end user. This I think has been damaging as it has only escalated the perception that these managers live in ivory towers and they speak a different language to the average Joe in the street.

Maybe by actually being able to converse with the end user greater faith can start to be restored in the investment industry.

Well there is light at the end of the tunnel. I was visiting a fund manager the other day who is developing a number of environmentally geared funds. Talking to one of their fund representatives I mentioned this subject and was pleasantly surprised that they had already arranged seminars directly with certain public groups.

I genuinely believe that it will be this sector that delivers change in this area.

And there is a final reason why this sector encourages you to see the effects of your investment and that's its involvement with communication technology.

THIS SECTOR IS MORE EMBRACING TOWARDS ADVANCING COMMUNICATION WITH YOU

You would have to be sitting on the planet Mars not to have noticed that means of communication are changing all the time. Just take a look at your kids. They don't phone anyone now. It's constant communication through text. They don't need to ring round all their friends to find out what's going on. They can just enter one of the many social network sites that they are members of.

These are the clients of the future and business will have to keep up. But I think that the financial services sector has fallen behind particularly with regard to contacting the younger client base. Strides are being made to change this and I think it's the new sustainability sector that is leading the way. Why is this? Well possibly because it is offering something different, new and exciting, and it needs to engage. It doesn't carry any of the rather staid stereotypes that the traditional investment industry still has, with social media in particular.

There have been some really exciting developments over the last few years. Let's look at some of these in more detail.

Firstly **e-commerce is becoming far more interactive** in the SRI sector.

Within the general financial services sector most organisations have websites. But I would question how engaging they are with you, the investor. Instead I feel many sites are quite complicated and leave you feeling detached from the organisation itself.

Organisations promoting SRI investing however are taking a lead in making sites more interactive. We have seen already how fund providers are engaging through blogs and forums inviting discussion on general environmental issues and views specific to funds.

There is also more interactive development with sites offered by intermediary organisations. One such site would be 'Blue & Green Investor' (formerly Worldwise Investor). This was launched in 2011 by Mark Hoskin, managing partner of an IFA 'Holden and Partners' and then taken over and rebranded by Blue & Green Tomorrow in 2013. The site in fact is aimed at both direct investors and other IFA's.

As well as offering up to date information on the SRI industry it offers a blog encouraging various parties to participate. Additionally it offers an on-line survey allowing the investor or the IFA, on their behalf, to establish which investments suit their particular ethical stance.

Additionally the SRI sector is embracing other forms of social media. Organisations like the EIA for example are active in promoting SRI through Twitter and Linked-in.

There are also examples within the SRI field of communication benefitting from a mix of traditional media with newer technologies.

One very good example that I have come across is the 'Blue & Green Tomorrow' online magazine. Launched a few years ago this targets that part of the population that is interested in the ethical, and sustainable movement, and has disposable capital to invest.

Subscribers receive a fortnightly e- magazine together with specific printed reports that come out. They also allow IFA's to subscribe to a service which feeds them enquiries from the investor readership. Therefore they are more directly involved in promoting SRI investment.

So to sum up seeing what is happening with your money is important in achieving a successful investment. However seeing isn't the whole story. As we have seen in the past it's possible for people to distort what you see. It's therefore equally vital that you have trust in what you are investing in.

So does healthy sustainable investing offer trust. I think it does.

CHAPTER **FIVE**

YOU CAN PUT MONEY INTO SOMETHING YOU CAN TRUST

LET'S GET DOWN TO STARK FACTS HERE. IF you are investing your hard earned money in your pension or your children's future then why should you bother if you have no faith in the system. I feel the same way with my investments, and I meet people all the time who are just reluctant to go anywhere near the stock market. The trouble of course is that the longer people avoid it the more confidence they lack. It's a never ending spiral. So trust is vital if you want to start having faith in investing again.

As we have already seen SRI investing is built on this trust.

Therefore I believe it can change people's views on investing. Before going into this let's establish a little more clearly why this breach of trust has been broken.

Not surprisingly surveys have shown that consumer confidence in the investment industry is at an all- time low.

For example the latest bi-annual Lloyds TSB Banking survey claimed that investor confidence is at its lowest ebb since the height of the 2008 financial crisis with only 25% confident in stock market prospects over the next year.

Then of course there is the statistical evidence provided by the markets reflecting this lack of trust. Over the last 10 years or so we have been hit continually with market crashes. From the dotcom bubble to the fraud exposures, to the banking crisis, time and time again the market, and more importantly your investment, has taken a nose dive.

An interesting statistic has come from the Barclays Capital Equity Gilt Study which measures the performance of the stock market against the Gilt market, which is government loan-stock in the UK. It measures this over a number of successive, rolling, 10 year periods stretching right back to the early years of the 20th century.

For the 10 years ending 2009 and 2010 the stock- market had underperformed gilts for only the 3rd and 4th time over this entire period.

Is this purely a reflection that the market is more volatile now and reacts to the way that news is now communicated? Undoubtedly this is an issue. However, despite some misinterpretation, journalists can only report on what has actually happened. If we hadn't had a series of serious economic and management scandals there would have been nothing substantial to report. If certain financial institutions hadn't been allowed to build up huge piles of toxic debt disguised as real profit it's unlikely the news filtering through would have been so bad. If these real events hadn't actually happened it's unlikely that stock markets would have fallen between 40- 50% at the end of 2008.

The point here is that trust was broken. We were encouraged to put our money or faith in investments that were not interested in sustainability. And the system was so lacking in transparency that nobody could see the effects of crooks who were just interested in their own greed.

The crash at the end of 2008 was particularly damaging because it was a systemic failure. In other words a whole industry was tarnished and corrupted. However it is also worth reminding ourselves that breaches of trust can be company specific and damaging in themselves.

The effects of the downfall of Enron and Worldcom were stark. As a result the markets fell drastically.

This time it was to do with false accounting and collusion, although of course ultimately greed. Again who would have wanted to invest in the stock market in the aftermath of these events?

It's worth noting that as a result of the above immediate corrective action was taken. Improvements were made to the whole system of company accounting and the term 'corporate social responsibility' was reborn. This has helped to restore some faith. This is perhaps a positive thing to come out of a stock market crash; the fact that lessons can be learned and that the economy can run more ethically than it was before.

This is an interesting point as in many ways I see the growth in environmental and socially responsible investing as a side effect of the systemic market failure that we experienced in 2008. Certainly there is a realisation that we have to invest in real things that actually improve people's lives. Investing in clean energy, water management and improved healthcare would surely come under this category.

So there has definitely been evidence to suggest that a succession of market failures has reduced people's confidence in investing.

But equally if confidence is undermined by negative events then the converse tends to apply. In other words if investors see positive action being taken then confidence will rise. The more often trust in an investment is strengthened the greater this confidence will become.

In other words **trust builds momentum for you as an investor**

As well as statistical evidence tending to point towards this conclusion there have been considerable psychological studies carried out in this area. Over the last few years there has been the emergence of a new school of thinking known as 'Behavioural Finance'. The main premise behind this is that people's decisions to invest are influenced a lot more by emotive factors than we have considered in the past. The proponents of these new theories argue that rather than get hung up on how their funds have performed over the last 12 months investors are influenced more heavily by the more basic emotions: for example fear, responsibility, and significantly here, trust.

In 2011 Professor Shlomo Benartzi of the University of California produced a report called 'Behavioural Finance in Action'. In it he argues that establishing greater trust is a key driver for improving financial confidence and outcomes for clients. A particular behavioural skill that the adviser should use is being open and honest about investment performance. To go on further he explains that advisers should be willing to discuss downturns as well as upturns. He also goes on to say that advisers should admit luck when performance exceeds expectations.

I would argue that managing client's emotions this way would be a lot easier for the adviser if he or she had faith in the underlying investments themselves. I believe that the further development of SRI funds, with sustainability at the core, will provide a sounder springboard to create these outcomes.

This is because sustainability at its core is more concerned with longer term performance and is not so hung up with shooting the lights out in the short term.

It's difficult to be precise on where long term starts. Five years is often cited by advisers as being the crossover point. Whatever the case it is clear that for a large proportion of society investing successfully over the long term will be key.

Therefore, where this is required, a good fund manager will want to make sure that he achieves healthy long term performance.

It is useful to understand this within the context of how markets behave. As we have seen from the FTSE graph in chapter 3 there is a lot of short term fluctuation. Often this is quite extreme and is often very strongly correlated to particular global events, be they political, economic, or financial.

These are often described as macro influences and are fuelled consistently by the mainstream media. In other words there is constant news flow creating speculation that creates volatility in the market, which in turn will have an immediate impact on share values.

However, as we have seen in chapter 3, the market has a habit of partially recovering pretty quickly. For example the FTSE closing price at 2nd January 2008 stood at 6416. Following the slump later that year the index fell as low as 3625 on the 2nd March 2009. By the 31 December 2009 it had recovered to 5312, in other words a 46.5% increase in the index from its lowest point. In my opinion this reflects the fact that macro influences can be quite short term. What then tends to take over are the micro influences, or the fundamentals as described earlier. These are the individual factors that determine a company's financial strength. In fact it's fair to say that rather than take over, these influences are there all the time, but are only clearly identified over a longer investment period.

Logically therefore if we recognise that a key fundamental for a company is its ability to manage its environmental and social sustainability then this offers a very encouraging message to the investor.

As we have seen throughout this book there is a mounting body of evidence to help support this argument. This is something an adviser can regularly communicate to their client.

As a result this can only significantly enhance investor's trust.

IN THE ENVIRONMENTAL SECTOR YOUR FUND MANAGER'S SUCCESS IS BUILT ON TRUST

So as we can see trust is vital for the success of your investment and in encouraging you to invest more; and as I touched on earlier the fund manager is aware of this need to be trusted. They know that their personal success will be hugely influenced by this trust.

Claudia Quiroz, fund manager for the Quilter Cheviot 'Climate Assets Fund', supports this view.

As well as ensuring capital growth on clients' capital she states the following, 'I additionally deal with very knowledgeable clients, making my job more exciting and more challenging. My clients understand the changes occurring in the market place and how a growing global population drives the demand for resources and the need to reduce carbon emissions. This means that I am much more accountable for the investment decisions that I make as my clients know very well the companies that are offering the right products and services to solve these sustainability problems'.

But this building of trust doesn't just happen by accident. It is a result of, I believe, a more thorough research process than has been the case in the past.

The genuine funds in this area are now combining traditional financial screening with wider social and environmental research. As a result they are digging much deeper into the heart and head of potential companies, and this is having positive results.

An example would be the Ecclesiastical Amity International

Fund which won the prestigious Lipper award in 2011 as the best global equity fund over 5 years.

A key element of the fund is that an in-house SRI team work alongside financial analyst colleagues. The SRI team will apply more rigid negative screens and then, more importantly, assess stocks on ESG factors, looking particularly where companies are sustainability leaders in their sectors. The financial analysts will then look at colder financial data, such as earnings quality and cash flow.

Both these activities tend to be primary screens, which will then be followed by company meetings. The combination of the financial and SRI perspective provides the basis for more insightful research to be carried out at these meetings.

This not only leads to more conviction buys but encourages greater engagement between the fund manager and the company executives. A good indicator of this engagement can be seen by the number of votes cast by Ecclesiastical, as a stakeholder, on company resolutions. Between April and July 2012 they voted at 119 meetings.

We now also see that this field encourages study, which is advancing the quality of fund research.

In this regard I have already mentioned the work of Buntz and Nguyen from Pictet who are looking at a more refined model for a quality sustainable investment. It was only by being in the environmental space that they were able to see how additional financial factors can work hand in hand with ecological governance to produce a successful stock.

This is not to say that the SRI area is completely bullet-proof from less trustworthy operations. From time to time advisers, like myself, will be pitched to by funds without the necessary credentials. These are often sold on the basis of some fantastic return but without the due diligence required to meet an SRI standard.

Reassuringly these are often spotted by professional advisers. Last year, for example, I was attending an EIA meeting and we were being pitched to by a prospective scheme representative. The scheme being sold was a reforestation project somewhere in South America. One of the audience asked the speaker whether the necessary care had been taken to respect bio-diversity when forests were being re-planted. For those of you unfamiliar with the term this is where the surrounding habitat, including plant and animal life is respected and preserved as best as possible. The pitcher had no idea how to respond. In fact it was obvious that he had no understanding of bio-diversity.

This is typical of many approaches where the pitchers completely misunderstand the motivation of their potential investors and try and lure people with financial returns only.

Therefore, as a potential investor it's always worth asking these questions, and if you are not sure speak to a professional SRI adviser.

So we can see that there is a real desire for fund managers to engender trust. But where is the source of all this trust. Ultimately it will depend upon the ethos of the company that you are investing in. It's worth remembering of course that these companies are simply formed of people like you and I.

COMPANIES IN THIS SECTOR SHARE YOUR GOALS

The evidence is fairly clear that the ethos of a company spreads down from the top. What motivates the CEO's of companies, and what action they take as a result, will affect everything that happens below it. Therefore it follows that if motivation at this level supersedes pure selfish financial motives and offers a real passion for making a difference to our surrounding habitat this will feed through the whole system.

Therefore I think it is highly significant that CEO's and entrepreneurs at the top of these ethical companies share the same passion as you for making a difference.

A good example would be Tom Werner. He has been the CEO of Sunpower since 2003, and has helped to build the company into a global leader in developing quality solar solutions for domestic and commercial uses. In particular he has helped to feed real passion and focus to the company. This has perhaps best been encapsulated in their Mission Statement, which states the following. 'Sunpower creates products, services and partnerships that provide world communities with a healthy planet'.

A clear indicator that these companies share your views is the fact that they engage more heavily with their stakeholders.

We have already seen that an important part of the fund managers' approach in this area is engagement. As a result the company executive has to be open to this form of engagement. They cannot be a closed shop.

Sunpower certainly takes this responsibility seriously. Not only do they engage directly with their investors and users they also encourage dialogue with a wider audience through thought leadership initiatives. One such initiative would be their 'Make an Impact' campaign, which encourages the advocacy of renewable energy ideas and education of key environmental issues via networks such as Facebook and Twitter.

CLEAR COMMUNICATION THAT BUSINESSES ARE RUN ETHICALLY IS IMPORTANT TO PEOPLE

We already saw in the last chapter how much better the environmental sector is at being transparent. But equally important is the clarity of information that is passed down.

By way of background the FCA (The Financial Conduct Authority) have recently laid down guidelines demanding that financial information is relayed in a way that is clear to understand and does not in any way mislead the investor. Well they have a job on their hands.

I am exposed to financial literature every day. Much of it confuses me and I have been in the industry for 25 years. God knows what it does to the man or woman on the street. This has not been helped by the ever more complicated product structures that have been coming out. The explosion in so called structured products is a fine example. In a nutshell these are where your return is dependent on certain events happening, bets on the market, to put it simply. People have become confused by these and the reams of paper that go towards explaining such structures.

My own experience tells me that people want a clear message as to how their money's invested. They are much more likely to buy if they can understand and associate with the asset concerned.

This helps to explain the growth in buy-to-let properties, as an investment, over the last few years. Despite having their pitfalls people were attracted to them because they felt they had some attachment.

I think the same could be said of SRI investments with the added factor that people can also associate to some extent on an emotional level.

It's important of course that the story behind SRI investing is communicated clearly. Evidence can be seen however that the facilitators are keen to make strides in this area.

One good indicator is the clarity of the fact sheets that are produced on funds in this area. Time is spent on actually explaining the underlying stocks, the companies that you're investing in, in other words. I would also suggest there is a move away from investment speak. This is a language devised only for investment fund managers to understand and will usually leave you, the investor, feeling glazed. Instead there is real effort to explain clearly where your money is going.

Another good indicator that clear information is being delivered is the fact that investors are communicating back by way of blogs and forums. It would be hard for individuals to do this if they didn't understand where they were investing in the first place.

So as we can see clarity of message increases trust. Conversely it is clear, particularly in light of the 2008 meltdown, that people will not trust complexity.

I have already mentioned above the confusion in the many structured products that have come on to the scene. But I think there is a more serious message behind this. Whilst in no way are all these products corrupt in themselves, they have helped to contribute to the mess we have created. What do I mean?

Well these structured products rely on derivatives and the build-up of these helped to fuel the massive increased demand for more of these derivatives. As we have seen this massive increase in demand made less scrupulous individuals cut corners. In a nutshell I believe the industry became too obsessed with making returns whichever way they could without thinking of the consequences of where they were investing. As challenging as it may sound to some I actually believe that the investment industry has a responsibility to help further a healthy economy in exactly the same way that you and I do. Why shouldn't they be able to tell us that their investment decisions are making a positive contribution?

So to sum up therefore a lack of clarity will more than often contribute to a lack of trust. So transparency and trust are vital elements in encouraging you to invest in a positive way.

There is a third element, and one which has been aimed at the SRI sector for some time. This claims that is there is a greater financial risk with these type of investments. On the contrary we have seen that by managing environmental and social risks it is likely that financial risk will be reduced. Having said this the SRI industry is not resting on its laurels and further strides are being made to reduce risk even further. I look at this in the next chapter.

CHAPTER **SIX**

YOU CAN NOW REDUCE RISK FURTHER BY SPREADING INVESTMENTS

ONE AREA THAT THE REGULATOR IS FOCUSED ON is the area of investment risk. Quite rightly so. As we have already seen there have been numerous occasions where investors have been left out in the cold by poor investment management.

So far in this book I have tended to concentrate on specific risks that apply to individual companies. As we have already seen risk at this level is now multi-faceted, including environmental and social risk. As a result those companies that manage all these risks together are much more likely to be long term winners.

However when considering an investor's entire portfolio we should also consider risk in a wider context. Evidence shows that we must also take into account the range of assets, such as asset class and asset size.

Furthermore, a criticism aimed at the SRI sector is that it doesn't have the range of assets to allow a well risk-adjusted portfolio. Well research is again proving this is not the case. On the contrary, this sector is now opening up to the full range of asset types, as well as some new ones. We will look at some of these later. In the meantime let's explore what we mean by a range of assets.

NOT ALL YOUR EGGS IN ONE BASKET

This is possibly one of the most well-known phrases used in financial services, and whilst it might sound a little jaded at times there is still a lot of validity in it.

It basically means you reduce your exposure to overall loss by spreading your investment around a number of different assets. Of course assets can mean any number of things. It can relate to the class of asset, to the size of asset, or even to its style. So basically some further explanation is required.

Perhaps the most important of these and certainly the element given most priority by the regulator, is the spreading of asset classes.

Before going any further let me clarify what an asset class is. I apologise if this is old ground for you, but it's important to understand fully what these are.

It basically refers to the category of investment you have placed your money in. The best way to expand on this is to provide a brief explanation of the main asset classes.

Shares: These are perhaps the best recognised type of asset. This is where you own a share of a company. They reward you by sometimes paying you income on the share (a dividend) and providing a capital return if the value of the share increases. Likewise you can lose money if the share price falls. Usually you will indirectly own a basket of these via a fund.

Corporate Bonds: Instead of owning part of the company this is where you lend money to a company. As with any loan they promise to pay the capital back at the end of the term, along with interest during the loan's duration. Because it's a loan you are promised to get a return, unlike a share, and therefore it carries less risk. There is some risk however because a company can go bust and the loan defaults. Again most funds would offer you a basket of these.

Gilts: These are similar to corporate bonds but where instead of lending to a company you are lending to a government. They are usually deemed to be one of the lowest risks because you would hope they don't go bust. This does of course depend on the government involved.

Property: Many pension and investment funds invest in property. This will by and large not be residential property but commercial. In fact the shopping centre you just walked through is probably owned by a pension fund. Returns here can be secured both by income from rent as well as hopefully capital through increased property values. Again of course you can lose money if the value of the property falls.

So there you have it. There are lots of variations of course, but this is the basic list.

It is generally accepted that if you wish to have a fairly balanced risk to your investments then you should have a mix of these assets in your portfolio. There is a lot of good evidence to back this up. For example if you look back over investment cycles you will often find that periods where shares have not performed well will be balanced by the fact that bonds have held up strongly. There are not always such clear correlations and I would not wish to enter this arena now. Needless to say overall performance of asset classes does jump around.

Opposite is a piece of evidence extracted from a graph, produced by fund manager Seven Investment Management. This shows the top performing asset classes over the last 5 years. It also shows the aggregate growth attributed to each asset class for the year. The bottom row also shows the worst performing asset class for each year.

2008	2009	2010	2011	2012
Global Govt. Bonds 50.7	Emerging Equity 64.1	Private Equity 41.1	Index Linked Gilts 19.9	Private Equity 25.7
Gold 42.8	Private Equity 47.6	Gold 34.7	Gilts 15.6	UK Property Shares 25.4
Emerging Mkt. Bonds 22.5	UK Equity 30.1	Emerging Equity 23.9	Gold 10.3	Emerging Equity 17.4
Timber 9.5	European Equity 18.3	Commodities 21.8	Emerging Mkt. Bonds 9.8	Corporate Bonds 15.6
Gilts 7.4	US Equity 14.5	US Equity 19.2	Global Govt. Bonds 8.0	European Equity 14.8
(Private Equity) (-64.3)	(Global Govt.Bonds) (-7)	(Timber) (-0.8)	(Emerging Equity) (-18.1)	(Commodities) (-5.4)

Govt. means Government and Mkt. short for market.

It is noticeable that the relative performance of asset classes varies significantly from one year to another. In fact, in certain cases, assets which appear in the top five one year are the bottom performing sector in another year. But spreading risk goes beyond this. As well as it making sense to spread asset classes many portfolio managers are recognising the importance of spreading size and style within each asset class. Better structured portfolios will now take note of this. For example, if they are looking at the UK stock market they will have exposure to small, medium, and large companies. They are also likely to identify different characteristics within these investments. The smaller companies, for example, may well be geared more for growth only, whereas the bigger companies may be seen as more of a safe haven from which income, in the form of dividends, is paid.

To conclude, spreading investments is still important. I suppose the most damming evidence of this would be where your investments plummet due to all your eggs being in one basket. The dotcom bubble provides a stark example. In other words, if at the turn of this century you happened to be invested purely in emerging high tech internet stocks there was probably a fairly good chance you would have got your fingers burned. In equal measure, there is a similar argument to say that you don't necessarily want to invest purely in renewable energy shares. As we can see however a SRI portfolio can now have a wide range to choose from.

There is now a much greater range of assets to invest in

In the past there has always been the criticism that the SRI universe is too marginal. It is argued that it doesn't provide you with enough investment choice to spread your investment.

However this arena has come a long way since Swampy-like figures were making hemp out of the back of cottages or wacky scientists were inventing their first wind generator. There is now a far more sophisticated range of holdings to choose from.

There is now a healthy range of asset classes that you can spread your portfolio amongst. No longer are you just looking at shares in recently formed companies. You now have access to the full range of assets. As well as equity funds, there are funds dealing in corporate bonds and fixed interests, property, as well as other alternative assets. In other words you can set up an investment to meet precisely with your overall risk profile.

This increase in the number of asset classes is again a reflection of the growth in the industry, and therefore will only continue to grow further. For example there are more corporate bonds available in the SRI market. Some of these will be from larger corporates who satisfy SRI screening. Equally there will be bonds issued by smaller companies who are becoming more developed and are now in a position to raise capital this way, as opposed to just issuing shares. As a result of this there are more and more bond funds being established.

There has also been growth in styles of investments within each asset class. This provides you with further diversification, which again helps to spread your risk. For example within the equity category you would have access to larger corporates that may tend to be a little more defensive in their nature. In other words they may be protected more in uncertain times within a certain sector. These will be present in 'Best of Sector' funds which tend to concentrate on companies that are leading the way in sustainability in their particular industry. The Ecclesiastical Amity International Fund, mentioned in the previous chapter, offers more this style of investment with holdings that include the likes of General Electric and Glaxo SmithKline.

You then can invest in more medium sized companies that perhaps have greater growth prospects. This can often be a feature of those funds that have particular themes. The Jupiter Ecology fund, again mentioned earlier, is a good example.

What's more you can now access all of these under one roof. There are funds of funds and portfolios that offer you a composite mix of all of these in one package.

A GROWING UNIVERSE

More significantly the sheer number and size of investable assets that these funds can invest in has increased rapidly. This is in direct response to the growth within the green and sustainable economy. Furthermore there is every sign that it will keep increasing.

Of course it's impossible to be precise on the sheer scale. This is because it is in some way subjective at which point we draw a line and say this company is making a positive contribution whereas this one isn't.

However as indicated earlier we have seen the emergence of specific stock market indices ring-fencing companies that are attempting a more sustainable mission. FTSE, for example have set up the FTSE4Good index, which measures companies in the global market that meet certain responsible criteria. As of March 2011 the index had 894 constituents, equivalent to 25% of the numbers in the FTSE World All-Share index. The US counterpart, the Dow Jones Sustainability Index, has been running even longer and as of September 2012 had 592 holdings, 8.5% of the general Dow Jones world index.

In addition to those recognised indices we are also seeing a big increase in investable stocks in the new powerful economies. China, for example, is now the largest wind turbine and solar PV manufacturer in the world.

And this trend is unlikely to halt. There will be more and more investments to choose from. As we have hinted at before this trend will only be encouraged by continuous stimulus from our governments. As we have already seen government expenditure is as high in this area as it has ever been and is continuing to move in an upward curve.

But it's not just the numbers that have been increasing. What's important from a risk point of view is that the variety of industries you can invest in has expanded. This is important for you because as we saw earlier diversification this way spreads your risk. We don't want to fall into the dotcom scenario and there is no reason why this should happen.

And again the growth in the variety of industries is a direct reflection of the growth in the sustainable economy as a whole. In fact there are so many areas the future looks pretty exciting. In order to aid your stimulation I have collated these into three very broad areas.

Firstly there are what I call the primary Eco industries.

By these I mean all those companies who are directly involved in meeting our major ecological challenges. These would include the following:

Climate change - Alternative energy

Resource management - Reducing our dependency on finite energy supplies

Water management - Preserving our water supply

Energy saving - Involved in energy management projects

Forestry - managing forests in a sustainable way and reducing global warming

Sustainable agriculture - Making more effective use of agricultural resources

Waste management - Reducing landfill and the resultant emissions

Then I would refer to the primary Social industries. There are now companies involved in all of the following:

Transport - This could be eco as well but involved in providing more sustainable and less congested transport systems.

Health and well-being - Involved in improving the quality of peoples' lives.

Social housing - Improving the quality of communities.

Finally there is a category I would refer to as subsidiary industries.

These are the companies that supply things to these primary industries. This is a very important category and one that is often forgotten. Having access to these provides even more diversification for you.

BETTER PROCESS FROM FUND MANAGERS

From a fund manager's perspective it's not just about putting the right spread of companies into its fund. The process by which this fund is managed is also vital. In this regard I think the management process in the sustainable sector has stolen a march on its conventional counterpart.

We have already seen how there is far greater research into the analysis used in constructing a fund, both SRI and financial. Consequently they will be monitoring a far greater depth of information as they run the fund, compared with the average fund manager.

In addition managers will be accessing a far greater range of research based theory helping them to improve the risk adjusted returns of their funds. The study from Buntz and Nguyen, mentioned earlier is one example. Funds in this area also have the advantage of benefitting from EIRIS, an independent research organisation who has been set up to support the industry, in part to pass on research based theory. EIRIS has a multi-national team, who work with a global network of SRI specialists around the world. According to the latest figures from their website they are working with over 100 institutional and retail funds.

A better flow of information is also likely to lead to better quality engagement between the fund manager and their stocks. Better engagement will then lead to better decisions being made by company executives, so we have a continuous circle of improvement being created.

Engagement will come in many forms. It can be in a more formal way such as voting on certain resolutions. We saw in the last chapter how funds like the Ecclesiastical International Fund have been very pro-active in this regard. It can also be more regular contact in a more direct sense.

OUTSIDE INFLUENCE

Fund managers in this area also often benefit from a greater range of outside influences. This is often in the form of external specialists who are able to offer a particular insight into ESG risks. This extra layer of oversight also helps to reduce the possibilities of risk.

In some cases this will be more ad-hoc. For example, the fund manager Pictet often rely on research from external environmental agencies. However the influence can often be more formal. The F&C Stewardship fund, for example, has a 'Committee of Reference'. This is a committee made up of external and independent members that has to approve of each stock that the fund wants to take on. Whilst some may consider this to be an unnecessary hurdle F&C believe that this adds an extra layer of control and expertise. The current committee, for instance, includes John Elkington, founding partner and director of Volans, a company supporting entrepreneurship at the cutting edge of sustainability. It also boasts Jiggy Lloyd, an independent consultant in public policy and sustainable development, who in the past has held senior positions with large environmental organisations, such as Generale Des Eaux and Severn Trent.

AVOIDING BENCHMARKS

Interestingly SRI funds can often improve their risk adjusted returns by not being restricted by the so called 'benchmark'.

In short, benchmarks have come about because it was considered important to measure the performance of certain funds against each other. As a result funds that are deemed similar in their

make-up are grouped together and measured against a set
benchmark. This benchmark, in other words, tends to represent
the average make-up of these funds.

A good example of this would be the 'Balanced Managed'
benchmark. A typical balanced managed fund will have a mix of
asset classes within it. For example, it can hold anything
between 20% and 60% in shares. A fair amount of these shares
will also typically be larger, blue chip UK stock.

The problem is that once you have this benchmark funds don't
want to stray very far from this. It then becomes a millstone
around the neck and there tends to be a herd mentality where
funds tend to adopt similar more restrictive styles.

The beauty with many SRI funds is that they don't sit very easily
within a category. Therefore they tend not to have a benchmark.
This in turn gives more freedom to the fund manager and means
he can really follow his convictions, backed up by research of
course. Feedback suggests fund managers like working with
conviction because they can avoid risks that their research is
throwing up.

To summarise, better informed risk management can now be
added to the list of positive factors attributed to SRI investing.

In other words, you can now achieve a positive environmental or
social impact and make a risk-adjusted sustainable return. You
can achieve this with a degree of trust and transparency that you
may not have experienced before.

Having said this SRI investments are still subject to financial
risk as with more conventional funds. They don't escape this.
Therefore the same risk assessment should be carried out on an

investor looking to invest in SRI, as with any other fund, before a recommendation is made.

As SRI is still a relatively new concept in the investment world it may be unrealistic to expect you to suddenly change all of your investments. The mainstream is still called the mainstream for a reason, and investments with an ecological or social slant to them are still in the minority.

I, for example, am still exposed to the mainstream market with a number of my funds. However I have decided to place some of my holdings in the SRI space.

Why?

Because I think if everybody does the same it could make a significant impact.

Read on.

CHAPTER **SEVEN**

YOU DON'T HAVE TO PLACE 100% IN THIS SPACE TO MAKE A DIFFERENCE

WE HAVE ALREADY SEEN THAT RESPONSIBLE INVESTING IS becoming more widespread. This after all is just a reflection of what is happening in the outside world. However there is still a large part of the investment market that doesn't see influencing positive change as its role.

As a result you and I have to be realistic. Is it feasible that we can invest all our savings in funds that have specific environmental and social remits? I say probably not. For example. that is the case with my own investments.

At this moment I have invested between 30- 40% of my disposable capital this way. You can make a difference by placing just 10 % in SRI funds.

Why is that? Four reasons I can think of

EVERYBODY'S 10% IS MORE INFLUENTIAL THAN A FEW WITH 100%

Take any every-day product or service that we now take for granted. You can draw a line from when it was a marginal product to when it became mass market, when it was accepted as the norm.

Take car production at the turn of the century. In the early years the car was very much seen as a toy for the very wealthy. Indeed it wasn't until the 1950's that car use became more the norm in the developed world.

However certain changes happened along the way which allowed the change from marginal to mainstream to happen. Instrumental in this was Henry T Ford and the start of the mass production line. The first Model T came off the production line in 1908. By 1927 15 million had been produced. For the first time cars could be assembled relatively cheaply so that they could enter the range of the non -mega wealthy.

Imagine if this had not happened and the car had just continued to be made in specialist workshops for rich enthusiasts.

Therefore it's when the mass market becomes interested in something that a product or service really starts becoming influential.

A more recent phenomenon in the investment side has been the rise of buy-to-let investments. 20 years ago the thought of investing in residential property and letting it out was not considered normal. This was the terrain of specialist property developers. Nowadays provided you have a reasonable deposit and credit record, anyone can enter the market. Again certain triggers happened that allowed this change to happen. There was consumer pressure to make this type of investment more accessible and the mortgage industry made financing deals more readily available and attractive.

In other words it went from the margins to the mainstream by more people entering the market.

And so the same story can apply with responsible investing. Everybody entering and putting 10% in this space will have far more effect than continuing to rely wholly on the more extreme investor.

That is not to say that the more specialist, extreme investor has not been vital. They have helped to put this concept on the map. It's just that to spread the influence it has to become the norm.

And your 10% not only makes the market grow quicker it provides the industry with more credibility.

In other words, by more people showing they can invest and support the environment, the more this will make sense to the investment industry.

Ideally it would be great if every single investment considered its impact on the outside world and recognised that it could influence change. I believe this can happen eventually.

But in order to get there you and I need to put your toe in the water now.

A good analogy is that of the recycling industry.

15 years ago domestic recycling was seen generally as an activity of the eco warrior. However pressure and legislation forced everybody to get involved. Initially many considered having to sort out certain rubbish and fill up a certain bin as being a right chore. However now most people not only have got used to it but they thoroughly embrace the idea, and even pour scorn on those that don't. Recycling, in other words, is now seen as a totally credible industry.

Finally simple maths applies to this theory. If everybody puts in 10% that will direct far more money to ecological and social change than is currently the position.

If you don't believe me let's have a look at the facts in the UK. According to the IMA –Investment Management Association the total UK investment in retail funds in 2012 was £597bn (retail funds being investment funds bought on the market by individual investors).

10% of that figure would therefore be £59**bn**

This is compares with the total £11**bn** which was actually invested in green and ethical funds at that point.

YOU WILL BUY INTO A CONCEPT IF COMMITMENT IS REALISTIC

Let's say you suddenly expressed an interest in keeping fit. As a result you decided to get heavily into cycling, as you would not only achieve greater fitness but have great fun doing it.

Would you then go and spend all of your disposable income on a bike and necessary accessories. Would you cut out everything else just to cater for this new activity? The answer is likely to be no.

You would not suddenly decide to stop going to the cinema, to stop shopping for clothes, to pop down to your local and a have a few pints with your mates. Well I know I wouldn't.

In other words it's unrealistic to expect you to throw everything at a new commitment.

The same principle applies with your investments. We know that investing in areas that stimulate our environment is vital, but we also know that this needs to be balanced with mainstream investments. Those investments that, for now, do not portray such a clear objective.

If we break this down more logically, investment in the responsible investment sector will simply mirror our overall proportionate spend in these sustainable areas.

A good exercise for example would be to take your average monthly spend on food and everyday household items. Then calculate the proportion of which is environmentally or socially sustainable.

I have carried out that very exercise and discovered that my proportionate spend comes out at around 10%. Yours may be similar. You see my point.

Looking at it from another angle certain product areas will only remain financially sustainable if consumers continue to spend money on them in the long term. Chocolate biscuits are a good example. Like many other people my family enjoy chocolate biscuits, and whilst not offering any explicit social and environmental benefit, we see them as a little luxury adding to the quality of our lives. It would be fair to say there are a number of household products that fit into this category.

To use the biscuit example, if we all suddenly start becoming obese and contracting strange illnesses then society might start to take an alternative view. However it is reasonable to accept for now that society can take a balanced view. In other words it can recognise that there is a place for these products, as long as a certain line isn't crossed.

As a result, it is reasonable to expect investors to see buying opportunities in companies that manufacture these products.

Following on from that is the point that

GOOD VIBES START GOOD HABITS

With any new type of consuming it takes time to get used to it, and eventually become comfortable with it. Let's continue with the area of sustainable household products. In particular think of an ethically sustainable product that you buy all the time now.

I'm going to pick Fairtrade coffee. Believe it or not when I first took the mammoth step of buying Fairtrade I deliberated long and hard on why I should spend more money on coffee. This was the first step, putting my toe in the water. Having made that momentous decision, I then discovered what an enjoyable experience it was drinking quality coffee in the knowledge that I was also improving the social environment of those coffee farmers from developing nations.

I then started researching a little bit into the Fairtrade mark, now recognised as a quality endorsement of ethical and environmental practice. This then stimulated me to look more closely at other products to see where and how they were produced. This was the second stage. Good vibes had started good habits.

Now there are several grocery products that we tend to buy which meet these objectives. However it's worth stating that I'm no eco warrior. I don't buy shirts made from hemp. There is still a balance.

Maybe though the balance is shifting towards a more supportive sustainable environment. The same I believe will happen with the investment world.

If we start to invest maybe 10% now in a more positive way I believe we will start to see benefits, and this will encourage us to put in a bit more. You see, good vibes start good habits.

There is a final reason why a realistic commitment is more sensible in the investment market.

That is you will be **less afraid of entering the market.**

A criticism often aimed at our society is that we don't like change. I would rephrase this and say we don't like quick change. In the UK, in particular, we like to put our toe in the water first and weigh things up before taking a plunge.

Take my earlier example of the emergence of the motor car. In the early years of mass manufacture did every single household go out and buy 2 cars, one for work, one as a run- around? I think not. Cars would eat up a huge proportion of the average disposable income in those days and in fact were not taken up by the majority until the 1950's

People are therefore wary about entering a new market. This is no different with a new investment sector.

There are still a lot of unknowns in the SRI sector. For example we still are unsure of how successful certain renewable energy production will be. We do know however that we will need alternative energy. Therefore it makes perfect sense to enter the market with some caution.

Leaving aside the emotional aspects, exposing your 10% will make it…

A MORE EFFECTIVE INVESTMENT FOR YOU BECAUSE IT'S SPREAD WITH OTHER AREAS

We need to feel comfortable with our investments.

Earlier we saw that sustainable funds do offer a considerable range of asset classes and types. However it would be unfair to suggest that currently, it can totally satisfy someone's overall attitude to risk.

One of the most important aspects when deciding where you

invest your money is your attitude to risk. But risk is not always an easy thing to measure. It has many dimensions. It can include how comfortable you are seeing your savings and investments fluctuate. It can also mean how much loss you are prepared to face when it comes to investing your money. It can vary between the short term and long term. All this is forgetting any environmental risk you wish to take with your overall investments.

For now however let's concentrate on the financial risks.

It's likely that with most people the analysis of risk on their overall wealth will not be clear cut. For example, short term investments may need to a carry a lower risk than those invested over a longer term. Often however, the overall assessment will demand a spread of all asset classes, ranging from cash deposits to share-based investments. Each asset class will then meet a particular need. For example, the cash is there to meet short term expenditure and emergencies and will therefore need to be safe.

Because most people require this spread it would be unrealistic to expect all of this to come from the SRI space. This is because SRI bias is still quite new in certain investment areas. For example, it's still pretty difficult to benefit from positively screened cash deposits, and it would be unfair to expect people to move in droves from the well-known high street banks.

Also you could make a distinction within the asset classes themselves. For example many SRI stocks, as we have seen, show great prospects for the longer term. This is perhaps particularly true of renewable energy or energy management. Therefore if you are looking to invest say over a 10 year period these could be a suitable bet. However if you were looking at around 5 years you might favour more defensive stocks. In other words companies that are less vulnerable to external market pressures over the shorter term. These could include utilities and pharmaceuticals, and possibly even banks.

Of course some of these stocks may well show positive environmental credentials, and if not that then at least they may be fairly neutral from an SRI point of view. There is perhaps an argument to say that this is acceptable if it provides security for that chosen investment period, and as a result liberates you to invest more sustainably over the longer term.

It might even make sense to tie this different criterion in with certain investment objectives. For example, funding for your daughter's wedding might require a more defensive investment if it's due in the next few years, whereas investing for your grandchildren might coincide well with longer term sustainable funds. This might resonate very strongly with you if you consider the positive impact it will also have on your grandchildren's world, when they grow up.

So again, provided it meets with your risk profile, it makes perfect sense to put just 10% in the SRI space for now.

Eventually however SRI investing will become more the norm. There may even come a day when every single fund manager considers his or her environmental or social impact. But in order to do that this sector must grow in a sensible way; and in order to do that it needs your steady support.

In other words **it will grow more sustainably when your commitment is more sustainable.**

The last thing responsible investing needs is a massive bubble; for everybody to get excited, pour money in, and then when things don't go as expected, pour money out.

This happened to the dotcom bubble. When the World Wide Web was newly introduced, budding entrepreneurs jumped on the bandwagon at the end of the 90's. Companies started forming, not because of any workable business strategy but purely because they could offer it through the web. Investors then joined them on the band wagon, in the false knowledge that growing returns were almost guaranteed. In many cases initially they were, as soaring share prices were viewed by many through rose coloured spectacles.

Eventually however the fairy tale was over. Suddenly it became obvious that many of these companies were not making any real profit at all and we all know what happened after that. The bubble burst.

Of course there were some success stories from that era. But the high tech communication industry took some time to recover as a whole. It took some time before investors felt comfortable putting their toes back in the water.

It's important therefore that the same thing doesn't happen to the SRI sector, particularly when you consider how vital the outcomes are. Therefore steadily increasing support from a growing market base will be far more beneficial than a short term, ill thought out surge.

If you look at this from the company perspective it is fully endorsed by the research mentioned earlier by our friends Buntz and Nguyen.

Remember, they assessed that the long term success of companies in this sector was more likely to happen if they grew steadily and organically and not too quickly.

Don't forget also that you will have more engagement with these types of investment. So as more people like you steadily grow their investment so more dynamic will the engagement process become. Companies will have to pay far more attention to their stakeholders because there will be more of them. As engagement becomes more important any misguided self-interest will become more difficult to get away with. There is a real chance that the economy and society will be working in harmony to make the world a better and safer world to live in.

A pipe dream? Well it doesn't have to be.

In fact you can help to start a movement investing this way.

CHAPTER **EIGHT**

LEAVE A POSITIVE LEGACY BY BEING PART OF A MOVEMENT

SO IT CAN BE SHOWN THAT PUTTING IN your 10% commitment, along with everyone else, can make a real difference. This is because a real growing movement is starting. The more people that join, the more effective it becomes.

Imagine peering out of your office window and noticing a crowd of say 50 extremely vocal protestors. It will have an impact, but unless it's something very close to your heart it's likely you may return to your desk after a short while.

Now imagine the next day this crowd has risen to 5000. What response are you likely to have now? It's just possible you might pay a little more attention to what's going on. You may want to check how you feel about their protest.

I see this as a very good analogy of the development of SRI investing. As the number of people experiencing it increases so will it start to move from the margins to the mainstream.

The creation of this movement is significant for the following reasons.

IT CAN HELP SHAPE THE ECONOMIC AND POLITICAL LANDSCAPE

A movement can do this in several ways.

Firstly it can help to sway public opinion towards positive investing. We often hear the term public opinion, but what do we mean by it? I tend to see it as the point when something moves from being a marginal view to a mass view. Instead of something being seen as new and strange it is now seen as normal and acceptable.

And once public opinion kicks in change will happen at a quicker pace. Industry and government will start to take far more notice.

You can apply this to the acceptance of alternative energy on the continent. If you look at areas like Austria, Germany or Scandinavia public opinion is very much in support of renewables. This is because a movement was started many years ago. A movement supported by government and industry, but a movement that ultimately had to be adopted by people like you and I.

Although in the UK we are lagging behind the continent in this area, a co-ordinated positive movement towards adopting a more balanced energy supply will enable us to catch up.

A positive movement will also have specific influence on the government. Indirectly of course, government are always swayed by public opinion. Without paying attention to it they wouldn't win elections.

However, a growing number of investors supporting the environment have triggered our government into a number of specific actions.

For example without specific investment already being made into renewables and energy efficiency it is unlikely the government's new Green Deal would have come into play. This provides further financial incentives to those that are willing to make environmentally friendly improvements to their homes. Equally would the government's Green Investment Bank have been launched, supporting new businesses in this area, if some sort of investment momentum had not already been identified?

The two will go hand in hand. A growing movement will provide more encouragement to the government and vice versa.

More importantly, growing support here will help influence policy abroad. In other words, we can help shape international policy towards creating a more sustainable world.

There is already of course plenty of evidence to suggest that international legislation has been guided by growing movements. For example, much of the European legislation on carbon reduction and renewable targets has come about because the more influential continental countries know that new forms of energy generation work.

In addition emerging companies can see that new technologies work and have popular support, and therefore they are keener to adopt them themselves. The rapid rise in the solar industry in China is a testament to this.

A MOVEMENT ENCOURAGES MORE ENGAGEMENT

We have already seen that positively screened investments support much greater engagement between those making and those receiving the investment. This will only be strengthened by the number of investors increasing. This in turn will increase the collective influence of these investors.

Equally we have seen that fund managers in this area are very keen to represent the views of their investment public. They are a far cry from the manager we discussed earlier in the book, who felt that his investors had no interest in where their money was being directed.

Therefore it follows that as numbers get larger these fund managers will see it as their duty to seek even greater representation. For example, many funds already have external representatives sitting on advisory boards. As these funds become bigger then so it is more likely that you will start to have greater input from people representing the individual investor.

Also with greater engagement comes greater knowledge. People like you will start to acquire far greater knowledge of the companies that are shaping our future. With this greater knowledge you will then be able engage at a much higher level. In other words, the quality of dialogue between management and stakeholders will increase; and as the quality of dialogue improves then so will future decisions and direction made by those companies.

We have already seen evidence of where real quality engagement with all stakeholders has shaped great moves forward. Projects like the Vienna project, where all parties were encouraged to get involved with changing the direction of future energy policy.

This could be a real step forward for stakeholder engagement.

We have also seen that this sector has been keen to open up many communication channels, such as blogs, Facebook pages, forums, as well as the more traditional routes.

It follows therefore that if we are keen to be more pro-active about where we invest our money, we will want to communicate this through the many channels available. This will have the effect of further increasing public awareness. More people will be intrigued as to this new way of investing. They will want to know more about it.

But let's not forget the most important aspect of getting involved and starting a movement. That is to create a real sea change in the way we shape our environment.

WE CAN HELP INFLUENCE POSITIVE CHANGE BY BEING IN A GROWING MOVEMENT

History has taught us that as soon as issues start getting taken on as a movement then momentum grows fast and real change starts to happen.

In fact it can often be broken down into several stages. **Firstly** there will tend to be the pioneers. The people who will stand on a limb a bit. At first they, along with their ideas, might seem a little weird. **Secondly** however, they will start to gather support from more people, often from a different strata of society. At this point a movement is formed. **The third stage** is when that movement has gathered momentum and entered the psyche of the mainstream. In other words, the issues, originally seen as way out, are now seen as normal and acceptable to fight for.

There have been many examples in the past where this has improved society. Take for example the issue of women's rights. This is something we take for granted today, but as recently as the late nineteenth, early twentieth century this was certainly not the case.

The full vote for women didn't come about in fact until 1928. The origins of this change however can be traced back 50 years or so earlier. To be specific a lady called Lydia Becker formed the Manchester suffragette movement in 1867 following reaction to an article she wrote on the subject. As a result of the Manchester group being formed similar groups started springing up all over the country. A movement was formed and political pressure followed as a result.

Therefore it was only when the suffragette movement start to take shape that it attracted sufficient attention, and as a result real concrete change started to take shape.

A direct analogy can be made with the environmental and social movement to date. We have gone through the pioneer stage. We experienced the shock tactics of organisations like Greenpeace and the radical ideas put forward by Friends of the Earth. We now accept that those radical ideas are part of accepted strategy today.

I believe over the last few years we have moved into that second stage. We are all carrying out far more environmental and socially aware activities. We even have serious political representation in this regard and we are starting to realise the benefits of investing in this direction.

The challenge therefore is to move through the second stage and into the third. In other words to make positive investing the norm.

When we have reached that point then we will start to realise fundamental change.

By deciding to invest your bit this way you will help to create this sea change. And if you're still unsure just remind yourself where we are now compared with where we were say 20 years ago, even 10 years ago. Look at the strides we have made already.

In the developed world we are moving away from a throw-away society and towards one where we recycle and wrestle with saving energy.

We consider it sensible to assess the feasibility of solar panels on our house.

We quite happily buy cars which run partly on a battery.

We buy carbon offsets with our flights.

We will research ordinary everyday household products to check whether they were produced sustainably.

We will also check how healthy the food that we buy is for us.

We now readily accept that alternative healthcare should sit alongside the traditional pharmaceutical healthcare.

The list goes on.

So if these areas have become more the norm then would it not make absolute sense to continue investing in their development? Of course it would!

Have our lives not become richer because of these developments? Of course they have!

Is it not fair, humane and sensible that every part of the globe should benefit from these? Of course they should!

Will our economy be healthier and more successful as a result? It has to be.

Investing your bit now will start to force real sustainable positive change.

As a result there's just a chance you might feel good about it!

SOURCE NOTES FOR INVEST FEEL GOOD AND MAKE A DIFFERENCE

INTRODUCTION CHAPTER

Lloyds TSB Private Banking Survey January 2012   i

YouGov researched survey 2010 on behalf of UKSIF
(NEIW Week- National Ethical Investment Week)   i

United Nations Environmental Programme Report of 2012   iv

Based on SSE (Scottish and Southern) Annual Report June 2012
taken from www.sse.com   iv

M&S investor information from
www.corporate.marksandspencer.com   v

Funds under management grown in accordance with research from
EIRIS found on www.eiris.org   v

'Renewable Electricity Futures Study' report carried by National
Renewable Energy Laboratory 2012   vi

CHAPTER ONE

CHAPTER THREE

CHAPTER FOUR

CHAPTER FIVE

CHAPTER SIX

CHAPTER SEVEN

CHAPTER EIGHT

34446633R00086

Made in the USA
Charleston, SC
09 October 2014